PENGUIN PLAYS

PL49

THE LONG AND THE SHORT AND THE TALL

THE DUMB WAITER

A RESOUNDING TINKLE

The Long and the Short and the Tall

WILLIS HALL

*

The Dumb Waiter

HAROLD PINTER

*

A Resounding Tinkle

N. F. SIMPSON

PENGUIN BOOKS

Penguin Books Ltd, Harmondsworth, Middlesex, England
Penguin Books Pty Ltd, Ringwood, Victoria, Australia

—

The Long and the Short and the Tall

First published by Heinemann 1959
Published in Penguin Books 1961
Reprinted in this collection 1964
Copyright © Willis Hall, 1959

—

The Dumb Waiter

First published by Methuen 1960
Published in Penguin Books 1961
Reprinted in this collection 1964
Copyright © Harold Pinter, 1960

—

A Resounding Tinkle

First published by Faber and Faber 1958
Published by Penguin Books 1960
Reprinted in this collection 1964
Copyright © Norman Frederick Simpson, 1958

—

Made and printed in Great Britain by
Cox & Wyman Ltd, London, Fakenham and Reading
Set in Monotype Bembo

CONTENTS

WILLIS HALL

The Long and the Short and the Tall

THE LONG AND THE SHORT
AND THE TALL

Commissioned by the Oxford Theatre Group and first performed on the 'Fringe' of the Edinburgh Festival 1958, directed by Peter Dews.

The play was first produced in London on 7 January 1959 at the Royal Court Theatre. It was presented by the English Stage Company in association with Oscar Lewenstein and Wolf Mankowitz with the following cast:

465 SGT MITCHEM, R.	Robert Shaw
839 CPL JOHNSTONE, E.	Edward Judd
594 L/CPL MACLEISH, A. J.	Ronald Fraser
632 PTE WHITAKER, S.	David Andrews
777 PTE EVANS, T. E.	Alfred Lynch
877 PTE BAMFORTH, C.	Peter O'Toole
611 PTE SMITH, P.	Bryan Pringle
A JAPANESE SOLDIER	Kenji Takaki

The play directed by LINDSAY ANDERSON
with décor by ALAN TAGG

The action of the play takes place in the Malayan jungle during the Japanese advance on Singapore early in 1942.

ACT ONE

Time : Late afternoon.

The curtain rises on the wooden-walled, palm-thatched, dingy interior of a deserted store-hut in the Malayan jungle. The hut is set back a few hundred yards from a tin mine which is now deserted. There is a door in the rear wall with windows on either side looking out on to the veranda and jungle beyond. The hut has been stripped of everything of any value by the mine-workers before they fled – all that remains are a rickety table and two chairs, centre-stage, and a form, right.

> [*We hear a short burst of heavy gunfire in the distance – and then silence. A pause and then we hear the chirruping of crickets and the song of a bird in the jungle. A figure appears at the left-hand window, looks cautiously inside and ducks away. A moment later the door is kicked open and* JOHNSTONE *stands framed in the doorway holding a sten at his hip. When the door was kicked open the crickets and the bird ceased their song.* JOHNSTONE *glances around the room and, finding it to be unoccupied, makes a hand signal from the veranda.* JOHNSTONE *returns into the room and is joined a few seconds later by* MITCHEM, *who also carries a sten.*]

JOHNSTONE [*shifts his hat to the back of his head and places his sten on the table*]: All Clear. Stinks like something's dead.

MITCHEM [*placing his sten beside Johnstone's*]: It'll do. To be going on with. [*He crosses to the door and motions to the rest of the patrol.*] Come on, then! Let's have you! . . . Move it! Move!

> [*One by one the members of the patrol double into the room. With the exception of* WHITAKER, *who carries the radio transmitter/receiver on his back, the men are armed with rifles.* SMITH *carries Whitaker's rifle. They are tired and dishevelled.*]

JOHNSTONE: Move yourselves! Gillo! Lacas! Lacas!

> [*As the last member of the patrol enters the room* MITCHEM *slams the*

9

door. The men stack their rifles in a corner of the hut and sit gratefully on the floor. WHITAKER *takes off the 'set' and sets it up on the table.* BAMFORTH *shrugs off his pack, places it as a pillow on the form, and makes himself comfortable.*]

JOHNSTONE: How long we here for?

MITCHEM [*glances at his watch*]: Half an hour or so, and then we'll push off back. Better mount a guard. Two men on stag. Fifteen minute shifts.

JOHNSTONE: Right ... [*He notices* BAMFORTH *who is now fully stretched out.*] Bamforth! ... Bamforth!

BAMFORTH [*raises himself with studied unconcern*]: You want me, Corp?

JOHNSTONE: Get on your feet, lad!

BAMFORTH: What's up?

JOHNSTONE: I said 'move'! [BAMFORTH *pulls himself slowly to his feet.*] You think you're on your holidays? Get your pack on!

BAMFORTH: You going to inspect us, Corp?

JOHNSTONE: Don't give me any of your mouth. Get your pack on! Smartish! Next time you keep it on till you hear different.

BAMFORTH [*heaves his pack on to one shoulder*]: Alright! O.K. All right.

JOHNSTONE: Right on!

[BAMFORTH *glances across at Mitchem.*]

MITCHEM: You heard what he said.

BAMFORTH [*struggles the pack on to both shoulders. He speaks under his breath*]: Nit!

[*There is a pause.* JOHNSTONE *crosses to face Bamforth.*]

JOHNSTONE: What was that?

BAMFORTH: Me. I only coughed.

MITCHEM: O.K., Bamforth, Just watch it, son.

JOHNSTONE: Too true, lad. Watch it. Watch it careful. I've had my bellyfull of you this time out. You watch your step. Put one foot wrong. Just one. I'll have you in the nick so fast your feet won't touch the ground. Just you move out of line, that's all.

BAMFORTH: You threatening me, Corp?

JOHNSTONE: I'm warning you!

BAMFORTH: I got witnesses!

JOHNSTONE: You'll have six months. The lot. I'll see to that,

Bamforth. I'll have your guts. One foot wrong, as sure as God I'll have your guts.

BAMFORTH: Try. Try it on for size.

MITCHEM [*crosses to intervene*]: Right. Pack it in. That's both of you. [BAMFORTH *turns away from Johnstone.*] I want two men for guard. First stag. Two volunteers ... Come on, come on!

SMITH [*pulls himself to his feet*]: First or second – what's the odds ...

MACLEISH [*follows suit*]: It's all the same to me.

MITCHEM: Better stay inside. Don't show yourselves. Cover the front. If anything's to come it's coming from out there. [MACLEISH *and* SMITH *take up their rifles and move across to cover the windows.*] How's the set?

WHITAKER [*looks up from tuning in the radio*]: It's dead. Still dis. U/s. Can't get a peep. I think the battery's giving up. Conking out.

BAMFORTH: Now he tells us! Signals! Flipping signallers – I've shot 'em. Talk about up the creek without a paddle.

MITCHEM: You got any suggestions, Bamforth ...

BAMFORTH: Only offering opinions.

MITCHEM: Well don't! Don't bother. If we want opinions from you we'll ask for them. From now on keep them to yourself. Now, pay attention. All of you. We're sticking here for half an hour at the most. After that we're ... heading back for camp. [*A murmur of relief from the men.*] Anybody any questions?

EVANS: Can we have a drag, Sarge?

MITCHEM: Yeh. Smoke if you want. You can get the humpy off your backs. Get what rest you can. Your best bet is to grab some kip. It's a long way back. Another thing, you'd better save your grub. I make it we'll get back before tomorrow night – but just in case we don't, go steady on the compo packs. O.K.? [*There is a murmur of agreement from the men.*] I want to have a sortie round. Outside. See how we're fixed. Check up. Fancy a trot, Johnno?

JOHNSTONE: Suits me.

[*The patrol remove their packs and place them on the floor.* MITCHEM *and* JOHNSTONE *pick up and check their stens.*]

MITCHEM: Keep at it on the set, Sammy son. Have another shot at getting through.

WHITAKER [*puts on headphones*]: Right, Sarge. Don't think it's going to do much good.

MITCHEM: Keep bashing. Mac!

MACLEISH [*turns from window*]: Aye?

MITCHEM: We're having a stroll as far as the road. You're i/c. We won't be long. As far as we know there's nothing in the area for miles – but if anything crops up – I mean, if you should see anything – don't shoot. Unless you've got to. Right?

MACLEISH: Fair enough.

MITCHEM: Ready, Johnno? [*Johnstone nods and follows Mitchem to the door.*] And keep your voices down, the lot of you.

JOHNSTONE: Bamforth! That includes you!

BAMFORTH [*who has been delving into his pack*]: I heard!

MITCHEM: Come on.

[MITCHEM *opens the door and exits, followed by* JOHNSTONE. *We see them move past window and disappear down the veranda steps.*]

BAMFORTH [*throwing down his pack in disgust*]: The creep. The stupid nit!

EVANS: Johnno's got it in for you, boyo. He'll have your guts for garters yet. He's after you. Chases you round from haircut to breakfast time.

BAMFORTH: Flipping toe-rag! He wants carving up. It's time that nit got sorted out. When this lot's over – when I get back to civvy street – I only want to meet him once. In town. That's all. Just once. Will someone see me now and hear my prayers? If I could come across him once without them tapes to come it on! I'll smash his face.

EVANS: Go on, man! He's twice the size of you! You wouldn't stand a chance, tapes or no tapes.

BAMFORTH: What do you know about scrapping? That's how you want them when you're putting in the nut. Up there. Bigger than yourself. And then you wham 'em – thump across the eyes. Straight across the eyes and then the knee and finish with the boot. All over. Send for the cleaners.

EVANS: You wouldn't fight like that, Bammo?

BAMFORTH: You want to lay me odds? I'll take fives on that. What

12

do you know about it, you ugly foreigner? Get back to Wales, you Cardiff creep. Only good for digging coal and singing hymns, your crummy lot.

EVANS: Shows how much you know, boy. You want to see some real fighting, Bammo, you go to Cardiff on a Saturday night. Round the docks. Outside the boozers. More fights in one night than you've had hot dinners.

BAMFORTH: Country stuff, son. Country stuff. You haven't got the first idea. You ever want to see a bloke carved up? Proper. So his missis thinks he's someone else. You hand that job to London boys.

SMITH [*glancing over his shoulder from the window*]: Why don't you jack it in?

BAMFORTH: What's that?

SMITH: You heard. I said, give it a rest.

BAMFORTH: I never heard your name and number in this conversation.

SMITH: I'm just telling you, that's all. I've had about enough. Bloody southerners shouting the odds. Always shouting the odds. You're like the rest. One sniff of a barmaid's apron and you're on the floor.

EVANS: That's how you want a barmaid, Smudge.

BAMFORTH: Good old Taff! Show us your leek! Get him! Getting barmaids on the floor! And I always thought you were a presbyterian.

EVANS: Strict Chapel. Every Sunday.

BAMFORTH: Sunday's his day off. When he leaves the milkmaid alone. Tuesdays and Wednesdays he's going steady with a Eisteddfod.

SMITH: Come again?

BAMFORTH: One of them bints in a long black hat and bits of lace. Always singing songs. Every time you go to the pictures you see them on the news. Singing songs and playing harps and that. Hymns. Like being in church only it's outside. Dodgy move – so they can whip them up the mountainside for half an hour afterwards. Very crafty boys, these Taffs. You've got to hand it to them.

EVANS: Go on, man!

BAMFORTH: Straight up. It's straight up, son. Got any fags, have you, Taff?

EVANS: I thought you must be after something.

[EVANS *takes a packet of cigarettes from his trouser pocket and offers one to Bamforth as he crosses towards him.* BAMFORTH *takes the cigarette.*]

BAMFORTH: So what? As long as it's only your fags I'm after, you've no need to worry, have you, son? My name's not Johnno.

MACLEISH [*turning at window*]: Bamforth, why don't you pack it in? We've heard about enough from you.

BAMFORTH: Silence in court! Acting Unpaid Lance Corporal Macleish is just about to pull his rank! Don't it make you sick! Doesn't it make you want to spew, eh? Sew a bit of tape on their arms and all at once they talk like someone else. What's the matter, Mac? You chasing your second stripe already?

MACLEISH: Are you looking for trouble, Bamforth? Because if you are you can have it, and no messing.

BAMFORTH: Ah, shut up, you Scotch haggis! Dry up, boy! It's not your fault. All Corps are bastards, we all know that.

MACLEISH: Watch your mouth! As far as I'm concerned the tape's not worth it. Just remember that. As far as I'm concerned I'll jack the tape tomorrow to drop you one on. And that's a promise, Bamforth.

BAMFORTH: Go stuff your tape.

[EVANS *lights his cigarette behind dialogue.*]

MACLEISH: So just you watch your mouth.

BAMFORTH: Aw, come off it, son. Where I come from it's just a name.

MACLEISH: It so happens I don't like it.

SMITH: Drop it, Mac. He didn't mean no harm.

MACLEISH: I'm willing to accept his apology.

BAMFORTH: So what's the argument about? Here, Taffy, give us a touch, boy.

EVANS [*hands his cigarette to* BAMFORTH *who lights his own and passes it back*]: I don't see, Mac, what you got to complain about. Bammo's only having you on. Before you got that tape you moaned about Johnno just as much as the rest of us. More, perhaps.

SMITH: Just let it drop, Taff, eh?

MACLEISH: It so happens that I accepted the rank of Lance Corporal.

Having accepted the rank, and the responsibility that goes with it, I feel it's my duty to back up my fellow N.C.O.s. And that decision is regardless of any personal prejudices I might hold.

BAMFORTH: King's Regulations, Chapter Three, Verse Seventeen. The congregation will rise and sing the hymn that's hanging up behind the door of the bog.

MACLEISH: You're just a head case, Bamforth. You're a nutter. Round the bend.

BAMFORTH [*jumping up on chair*]: With the inspired help of our dear friend and member, Fanny Whitaker, who will accompany the choir on her famous five-valve organ. All together, please! The chorus girl's lament! [*Sings*]

My husband's a corporal, a corporal, a corporal,
A very fine corporal is he!
All day he knocks men about, knocks men about, knocks men about,
At night he comes home and knocks me!

[EVANS *joins Bamforth in the chorus.*]

Singing Hey-jig-a-jig, cook a little pig, follow the band.
Follow the band all the way!
Singing Hey-jig-a-jig, cook a little pig, follow the band,
Follow the band all the way!

WHITAKER [*glances up from tuning set*]: Pack it in, Bamforth.

BAMFORTH [*unheeding*]: Order if you please! Second verse. [*Sings*]

'Cause my little sister Lily has a stroll on Piccadilly,
And my mother has another on the Strand,
And my father's flogging charcoal
Round the Elephant and Castle,
We're the finest flipping family in the land!

[EVANS *joins Bamforth again in the chorus.*]

Singing Hey-jig-a-jig, cook a little pig, follow the band.
Follow the band all the way!
Singing Hey-jig-a-jig . . .

WHITAKER [*rising, angrily*]: Will you pack it in!

BAMFORTH [*jumps to floor*]: Hello! Our little blue-eyed signaller doing his nut now. That's all we wanted – him!

WHITAKER [*putting headphones on the table*]: Why don't you keep quiet, Bamforth man! I got something on the set!

BAMFORTH: 'Course you did, my old flower of the East. What was it, Sammy son? Henry Hall? Tune it up a bit – let's have a listen. Bit of music always makes a change.

WHITAKER: I told you – I got something coming through.

MACLEISH: You think it was the camp?

BAMFORTH: We're fifteen miles from base. He's not Marconi. This boy couldn't get the Home Service in the sitting room.

WHITAKER: I don't know what it was. I got something.

BAMFORTH: Fifteen miles from base! A doolally battery and ten-thumbed Whitaker i/c! What you want? A screaming miracle?

SMITH: Try them again, Sammy. Have another go.

MACLEISH: Try it on transmit.

EVANS: Tell them I'm coming home tomorrow night, boyo. Ask them in the cookhouse what's for supper. What's tomorrow? Friday! It's fish and chips!

SMITH: Do you think of anything except your stomach?

BAMFORTH: He's a walking belly.

[WHITAKER *sits down and replaces headphones. He picks up the microphone and adjusts the set.* BAMFORTH *and* EVANS *approach table.*]

WHITAKER: Blue Patrol ... Blue Patrol calling Red Leader ... Blue Patrol calling Red Leader ... Are you receiving me ... Are you receiving me ... Blue Patrol calling Red Leader ... Are you receiving me ... Are you receiving me ... Over. [WHITAKER *flicks switch to 'receive'. There is a pause during which we hear some interference – but nothing else.* WHITAKER *flicks back to 'transmit'.*] Blue Patrol calling Red Leader ... Are you receiving me ... Are you receiving me ... Over. [WHITAKER *again flicks to 'receive'. More interference. Whitaker turns down the set and removes the headphones.*] It's dis. I think the battery's gone again.

BAMFORTH: So what's the use.

WHITAKER: I got something through, I tell you!

BAMFORTH: That's your story, boy. You stick to it.

EVANS: Perhaps you imagined it, Sammy boy.

WHITAKER: I had something coming through!

BAMFORTH: Don't give us that. Got through! You couldn't get through a hot dinner, my old son. You couldn't get through a NAAFI tart.

MACLEISH: Why don't you wrap up, Bamforth.

BAMFORTH: Eight-double-seven Private Bamforth to you, Corporal Macleish. You want to come the regimental, boy, we'll have it proper.

SMITH: That will be the day, Bamforth. When you can work it regimental. The biggest shower since the flood, that's you. Fred Karno's not in it. When you start giving us the heels together I'll be commanding the Camel Corps.

BAMFORTH: Get your bucket and spade, Smudger, and I'll lay it on. This boy can work it any way at all. If I go creeping after tapes I'll get them.

EVANS: Corporal Bamforth, NCO i/c latrines. It's you who'll want the bucket, Bammo.

BAMFORTH: That's all you know, you Welsh rabbit. You'd be the first to suffer. I'll have you running round the depot like a blue house-fly. Report to my tent at 1600 hours. Extra duties. Gas cape and running shoes.

EVANS: And can I have a week-end pass?

BAMFORTH: You what! What do you think you're on? Your father's yacht?

SMITH: You get some kip, Taff. Dream of home. It's the nearest you'll get to Welsh Wales.

[BAMFORTH crosses to form, picks up his pack, punches it into a pillow and lies down. WHITAKER, who has been attempting to tune set, puts on headphones and switches to 'transmit'.]

WHITAKER: Blue Patrol calling Red Leader ... Blue Patrol calling Red Leader ... Are you receiving me ... Are you receiving me ... Come in Red Leader ... Over.

[WHITAKER switches to 'receive' and again attempts to tune in set. EVANS opens his pack and takes out a crumpled magazine. BAMFORTH glances across at Evans.]

BAMFORTH: What you got there, Taff?

EVANS: A book.

BAMFORTH: Two's up.

EVANS: I'll let you have it when I've finished.

BAMFORTH [*sitting up*]: What is it? Sling it across.

EVANS [*crosses and sits on form*]: My mother saves me them. [*He hands the magazine to Bamforth.*]

BAMFORTH: And you've been carting this around for days!

EVANS: Why not?

BAMFORTH: Here, Smudger! Seen this?

SMITH: What's that?

BAMFORTH: Taff's library.

SMITH: Yeh?

BAMFORTH: 'Ladies' Companion and Home.'

SMITH: Get on.

EVANS: My mother sends it to me every week. I'm following the serial. What's wrong with that?

BAMFORTH: And you've been humping this since we left camp? Well, flipping stroll on! That's all. Stroll on.

EVANS: Why not? I've told you. I'm following the serial.

SMITH: Any good, Taff?

EVANS: Yes. It's all right. It's interesting. There's this bloke, see. In the army. Second Looey. He's knocking about with this girl who's a sort of nurse in a Military Hospital. Only before they have time to get to know each other proper, he gets posted overseas.

MACLEISH: Very exciting.

BAMFORTH: I'm crying my eyes out.

SMITH: So what happens then, Taff?

EVANS: Thing is, see, she doesn't know anything about it.

BAMFORTH: He should have taught her.

EVANS: I mean about this overseas posting. He's supposed to meet this bint one night round the back of the Nurses' Quarters.

BAMFORTH: The dirty old man.

EVANS: Who's telling this story, Bammo? Me or you?

SMITH: Get on with it, Taff.

EVANS: I'm just coming to the interesting bit if you'll give me a chance.

BAMFORTH: Come on then. Give. Let's have it. I can hardly wait to hear how Roger gets on in the long grass.

EVANS: That's just it. He doesn't.

BAMFORTH: I knew there'd be a catch in it.

EVANS: He never turns up, see. Been posted. Special Mission. Got to blow up an airfield in North Africa.

SMITH: What? On his tod?

EVANS: Last one I had he'd been captured by a tribe of marauding bedouins. Savage heathens.

SMITH: Get away!

EVANS: And it finished up the last time with them tying him, hand and foot, and hanging him upside down above a blazing fire. In a sort of oasis. There was him, toasting away if you like, with the sweat dripping down off the end of his nose. And these white-robed bedouins is dancing round, waving carbines, singing heathen songs, and not a care in the world. That was how it finished up in the last instalment.

SMITH: So what happens this week?

EVANS: That's just it. I can't make head or tail of it. This week starts off with him and this here nursing bint having an honeymoon in Brighton. Posh hotel, made up to captain, fourteen days' leave, smashing bit of crumpet, and the weather's glorious. Doesn't make sense to me. I think perhaps the old lady slipped up and sent me the wrong one first.

BAMFORTH: She slipped up all right. When she had you. Marauding bedouins! You'll lap up any old muck.

SMITH: After you with it, anyway, Taff.

BAMFORTH: You wait your turn. I'm two's up. [*He flicks through the pages of the magazine.*] Here – this is the bit I like. Margaret Denning Replies. All these bints writing up 'cause someone's left them in the club.

SMITH: Read us one out, Bammo.

BAMFORTH: Here's a right one. Get this. 'Dear Margaret Denning, I have been walking out for six months with a corporal in the Army who's a very nice boy.' Well, there's a lie for a kick-off.

EVANS: What's she want to know?

BAMFORTH: 'I like him very much and we plan to marry when the war is over. Lately, however, he has been making certain suggestions which I know are wrong.'

EVANS: Certain suggestions!

BAMFORTH: 'He says I ought to agree if I love him. What shall I do? Ought I to fall in with his wishes or should I stand by my principles and risk losing him? I have always wanted a white wedding. Yours, Gwynneth Rees, Aberystwyth.' It's another Taffy!

SMITH: So what's she tell her?

BAMFORTH: Dear Miss Taffy, I am sorry to hear that you have had the misfortune to fall in love with a corporal. The next time he starts making improper suggestions you should kick him in the crutch and marry a private.

EVANS: It doesn't say that, does it?

BAMFORTH [*rises and slings the magazine at Evans*]: What do you think, you ignorant burk?

EVANS: Oh, I don't know . . . What do you reckon she ought to do, Smudger?

SMITH: Same as Bammo says.

EVANS: I don't know, really. I suppose you've got to wait until you're married, proper. I mean, it spoils it otherwise, they say. But if this bloke she's going out with is in the army, perhaps he's up for overseas posting himself. I mean, things is different when there is a war. You never know, do you? He might get pushed off overseas for years, perhaps. Then where would he be?

BAMFORTH: Same as you. Up the creek without a paddle.

EVANS: That's what I'm getting at.

BAMFORTH: Wrap up, boy! Look. Don't be a creamer all your life. Have a day off. You've got a bint yourself, have you? Back home?

EVANS: I've got a girl friend. Well, of course I have. You know as well as I do. You've seen her picture.

BAMFORTH: So when you see her last?

EVANS: Embarkation leave, of course. Over a year ago. Eighteen months about.

BAMFORTH: Eighteen months! Stroll on! For all you know she could be weaning one by now. You know what Blighty is these days, do you? It's a carve up, son. A rotten carve up. Overrun with home postings wallahs, sitting back easy, sorting out the judies from Land's End to how's your father. They've got it all laid on, son. We're the mugs in this game. It's a den of vice, is Blighty. Unoriginal sin. Poles and Yanks and cartloads of glorious allies all colours of the rainbow. Even the nippers look like liquorice-allsorts. They're lapping it up, Taff. You think the bints are sitting knitting?

EVANS: Mine's all right, boy. Don't you worry about that.

BAMFORTH: You mean you hope she is. You're a bloody optimist. She's probably up the mountains right this minute with a big buck Yank.

EVANS: Go on, man! She's not like that.

BAMFORTH: They're all like that. So why should yours be any different?

EVANS: Well, if anything was wrong I'd hear about it.

BAMFORTH: Famous last words. What gives you that idea?

EVANS: Her mother's my auntie.

BAMFORTH: You can't marry her then. It's disgusting.

EVANS: Not my real auntie. She lives next door but one to us at home. I only call her my auntie. They've been friends, see, her mother and my mother for ever such a long time. My father's brother married her cousin, that's all. I've called her my auntie since I was a little lad.

BAMFORTH: You make it sound like rabbits.

EVANS: All the same, if anything was wrong with her, my mother would write and let me know.

BAMFORTH: You hope.

EVANS: Well, of course she would!

BAMFORTH: Look, son. Do yourself a favour, eh? Don't give me all that bull. There's only one way to keep them faithful. And that's like Smudger. Marry them sharpish and leave them with a couple of snappers running round the drum. Keep them occupied. With three or four nippers howling out for grub they don't have time to think about the other. Right, Smudge?

SMITH: That's about it.

MACLEISH: I fail to see, Bamforth, what experience you've had on the subject.

BAMFORTH: Get lost, you Scotch haggis.

EVANS: How many you got, Smudge?

SMITH: Two.

EVANS: Boys?

SMITH: One of each.

EVANS: Boy and a girl. Must be smashing.

SMITH: What? Kids?

EVANS: Not only that. You know. Having home, like. You know, something to go back to – afterwards. Home of your own, I mean. Wife and family and home and that. Got a house of your own yet, have you?

SMITH: Bit of a one. Council. Up on the new estate.

EVANS: Go on!

SMITH: It's all right. Bit of a garden, not much, but it's all right. Better than nothing.

EVANS: Did you do any gardening, Smudge, before you came in the army?

SMITH: Not a lot. Few veg. round the back – cabbages and that, brussels, couple of rows of peas, one or two blooms. Not a lot. You know – the usual.

EVANS: I know what you mean.

SMITH: Always left the front. Made a sort of a bit of a lawn of it. Sit out on Sundays on it after dinner. Me and the Missis. Saturday afternoons sometime – when there was football on the wireless. Just big enough to sit on – two of you. Nice bit of grass. At least, it was. I suppose the kids have racked it up.

EVANS: You don't know. Perhaps the missis has been looking after it.

SMITH: Perhaps.

EVANS: Must be worse for you, I suppose. Being stuck out here. Not like the rest of us. Having a family to think about, I mean.

BAMFORTH: Well, don't let that get you down, Taff. By the time you get out of this lot your Cardiff bint'll have a couple running round to call you 'dad'. I heard they've just posted in a regiment of Gurkha boys to Wales. For special training. They'll give her special training if I know them. Couple from that stud should just suit you. They'll match your battledress.

SMITH: That'd give the neighbours something to think about, Taff.

EVANS: I'd give her something to think about if she did.

BAMFORTH: Don't be like that, Taffy. Allies is allies, my old son. No good having allies if you're not willing to share what little bit you've got.

EVANS: They wouldn't be no allies of mine, then.

BAMFORTH: You're not democratic, that's your trouble. Just think! I can see you now – nipping off to Chapel Sundays with a little Sambo clinging on each hand. Right up your street, is that.

EVANS [rises and throws magazine at Bamforth]: I'll be up yours, Bammo, if you don't give it a rest!

BAMFORTH: You and who else?

EVANS [crossing and playfully sparring up to Bamforth]: Just me, boy. You're just my size.

BAMFORTH: Come on then, you Welsh Taff! Stick me one on!

EVANS: All right! You asked for it!

[EVANS closes in on Bamforth and throws a punch. BAMFORTH grabs Evans's hand and twists it up and round his back. BAMFORTH flings Evans to the floor, grabs a foot, and twists it from the ankle.]

EVANS: Go steady, man! You'll break my leg!

BAMFORTH: You're an ignorant Welsh Taff! What are you? An ignorant Welsh Taff!

EVANS: Get off my leg, you rotten fool!

BAMFORTH: Say you're an ignorant Welsh Taff! Say you're an ignorant Welsh Taff!

EVANS: You'll break my leg!

WHITAKER [adjusting radio controls]: Something coming through again!

BAMFORTH [to Evans]: Tell them! Come on, tell them what you are!

EVANS: Will you let go, man!

BAMFORTH: Tell them what you are.

EVANS: I'm an ignorant Welsh Taff . . . I'm an ignorant Welsh Taff!

MACLEISH: Bamforth! Evans! Knock it off, the pair of you!

BAMFORTH [disengaging himself from Evans]: What's the matter now?

EVANS [*climbs to his feet*]: You want to go easy, Bammo boy. You damn near crippled me.

[BAMFORTH *and* EVANS *move across to where Whitaker is seated. The radio operator is again attempting to contact base.*]

WHITAKER [*flicking transmitter switch*]: Blue Patrol ... Blue Patrol calling Red Leader ... Are you receiving me ... Are you receiving me ... Over ... [WHITAKER *flicks to 'receive' and adjusts controls. He fades up the volume and we hear the crackle of interference on the set. For a moment there is also the sound of distorted speech on the radio – though the distortion and interference are too strong to make the voice distinguishable.*] It's there again!

EVANS: He's right, Bammo! I heard it myself.

BAMFORTH: Ah, so what.

EVANS: I heard voices, Bammo!

BAMFORTH: So what does that make you? Joan of Arc? What if you did? Could have been from any of the mobs up the jungle.

EVANS: Could have been base, boyo.

[WHITAKER *takes off the headphones.*]

MACLEISH: Could you make out what it was Whitaker?

WHITAKER [*shakes his head*]: Too much interference. [*He switches the set off.*] I'd better leave it. No sense in wasting the battery. I'll leave it now till Mitch gets back.

BAMFORTH [*crosses to form, picks up his pack, and takes out a food pack*]: You do that, son. You tell old mother Mitchem all about it. What a good boy you've been. Please, Sergeant, I've been working ever so hard. Please, Sergeant, I've been fiddling about with my little wireless all the time that you were out. Please, Sergeant, can I have a stripe? You make me sick. [*He tears open the food pack.*] Stroll on! Look here. Bungy. Bloody cheese again. I'll swing for that ration corporal one of these days.

EVANS: What do you reckon it was, Smudge?

SMITH: What's that?

EVANS: On the set. You think it might have been camp?

SMITH: Don't ask me. Whitaker's the boy to ask.

WHITAKER: Must have been. It's only fifteen miles to base. The nearest mob to us are nearly thirty miles up country.

EVANS: What the hell are we supposed to be doing anyway? Stuck here in the middle?

SMITH: Playing at soldiers. What they call a routine patrol, Taff. Keeping out of mischief. Out of the NAAFI bar. It keeps you under control. Keeps the Colonel happy. It's good for morale.

EVANS: It's no good for my rotten feet. These boots, I think. The rubber soles that draw them.

BAMFORTH: It's a crumb patrol. It's just about the crummiest detail in the Far East is this, and no messing. Two days humping kit and two days back! Routine Patrol! You can stick this for a game of soldiers. Talk about the P.B.I. If ever there was an all-time crumb patrol, we're on it. [*He glances round at* WHITAKER, *who has taken a needle, ball of wool, and a pair of socks from his pack and is busily engaged in darning.*] What the hell are you supposed to be doing? [WHITAKER, *bent over his task, does not look up.*] You!

WHITAKER [*looks up*]: What's up?

BAMFORTH: What are you on like?

WHITAKER: My socks.

BAMFORTH: What for?

WHITAKER: Kit Inspection Saturday morning.

BAMFORTH: Well, that just about beats the lot, does that. Now I've seen everything. Rotten stroll on! The third day's hump we're on – three days out and bright boy's sweating on a kit inspection! What with him and his 'Ladies' Companion' and you and your knitting! If the Japs ever get down as far as this they'll have you two grafting in their regimental brothel.

MACLEISH: And where will you be, Bamforth?

BAMFORTH: Me?

MACLEISH: When the Japs arrive?

BAMFORTH: Not here, that's certain. I wasn't meant to be a hero.

MACLEISH: I gathered that.

BAMFORTH: I'll tell you where I'll be, boy. Scarpering. Using my loaf. On the trot. I've got it all worked out. The lot. Tin of Cherry Blossom Dark Tan from head to foot. Couple of banana leaves round my old whatsits. Straight through Kew Gardens outside and head for the water. Like one of the locals.

EVANS: You reckon you could make it, Bammo?

BAMFORTH: What! If the yellow hordes were waving bayonets at me I'd be off like a whippet. You'll not see my tail for dust. There's more wog rowing boats up the coast than enough. Nip off in one of them and straight to sea.

SMITH: On your own?

BAMFORTH: Tod or nothing. When the time comes, Smudge, it's going to be every man for himself.

EVANS: Go on, man. Where could you make for?

BAMFORTH: What's it matter? Anywhere but here. Desert Island. One that's loaded with bags of native bints wearing grass frocks. Settle down and turn native. Anything's better than ending up with Tojo's boys.

EVANS: You'd never do it.

BAMFORTH: That's all you know. Come down the beach and wave me off. If you've got time to wave with all them little Nippos on your trail. I'll be in the boat, Jack. Lying back and getting sunburnt with a basket of coconuts. [*Cod American.*] And so we say farewell to this lush, green, and prosperous country of Malaya. As the sun sets in the west our tiny boat bobs peacefully towards the horizon. We take one last glimpse at the beautiful tropical coastline and can see, in the distance, our old comrade in arms and hopeless radio operator, Private Whitaker, making peace with the invading Army of the Rising Sun – and the invading Army of the Rising Sun is carving pieces out of Private Whitaker.

WHITAKER [*rising*]: Pack it in, Bamforth.

BAMFORTH: What's the matter, Whitto? Getting windy?

WHITAKER: Just pack it in, that's all.

BAMFORTH: Get knotted.

MACLEISH: I haven't seen anybody handing medals to you yet, Bamforth.

BAMFORTH: No, my old haggis basher. And you're not likely to. I've told you – I don't go a bundle on this death or glory stuff.

MACLEISH: So why not keep your trap shut?

BAMFORTH: Democracy, Mac. Free Speech. Votes for women and eight-double-seven Private Bamforth for Prime Minister.

SMITH: Show us your Red Flag, Bammo.

BAMFORTH: It's what we're fighting for. Loose living and six months' holiday a year. The General told me that himself. 'Bamforth,' he says to me, taking me round the back of the lav at Catterick, 'Bammo, my old son, the British Army's in a desperate position. The yellow peril's about to descend upon us, the gatling's jammed, the Colonel's dead, and the cook corporal's stuffed the regimental mascot in the oven. On top of all that, and as if we hadn't got enough to worry about, we've got two thousand Jocks up the jungle suffering from screaming ab-dabs and going mad for women, beer, and haggis. We're posting you out there, Bammo,' he says, 'to relieve the situation.' So before I had time to relieve myself, here I was.

MACLEISH: And what have you got against the Jocks?

BAMFORTH: Stroll on! He's off again! It's a joke, you thick-skulled nit!

MACLEISH: And I'll not stand for any of your insubordinations.

BAMFORTH: Come on, boy! Come it on! Pull the tape on me again. That's all I want. I'll blanco your belt for you for twopence.

MACLEISH: When you're on duty, Bamforth, you'll take orders like the rest.

BAMFORTH: Get the ink dry in your pay-book first. You've not had the tape a month.

MACLEISH: If I'm in charge here, that's all that matters, as far as you're concerned. It makes no difference to you if I've had the tape five minutes or five years. You'll jump to it, boy, when I'm calling out the time. You'll just do as you're told, or you're for the high jump. [BAMFORTH *swears under his breath and turns away*.] Bamforth! Bamforth, I'm talking to you!

BAMFORTH [*swings round*]: Private Bamforth! I've got a rank myself, Acting Unpaid Unwanted Lance Corporal Macleish!

MACLEISH: Evans!

EVANS: Corp?

MACLEISH: Come here. [*As* EVANS *crosses towards the window* MACLEISH *tosses him the rifle*.] Here. You're on guard. Take over from me.

EVANS: Corp.

27

MACLEISH [*crosses down to face Bamforth*]: I'm not giving you any second warnings, Bamforth. When you speak to me you'll watch your mouth. I mean that, Bamforth, just watch out – or as sure as I'm standing here, I'll have you.

BAMFORTH: Try taking off your tape and saying that, you Scotch get.

MACLEISH: I've already told you, this has got nothing to do with the tape. I'm not warning you for c.o.'s orders, boy. I'm not interested in having you on the c.o.'s veranda with your cap and belt off. One word to me and I'll put your teeth down your throat. I mean that.

BAMFORTH: What with?

MACLEISH [*raising his fists*]: These. Just these.

BAMFORTH [*unfastening his jacket*]: If you want to play it the hard way, Jock . . .

MACLEISH: I want to play it any way that suits me. And right now it suits me to sort you out.

SMITH [*crossing from window*]: Wrap it up, Jock.

MACLEISH: You keep out of this, Smudge. This has got nothing to do with you – it's personal between Bamforth and myself – it's got nothing to do with you.

SMITH: Like hell it hasn't. You're like a couple of kids.

MACLEISH: I said keep out of it!

SMITH: Grow up! For God's sake grow up the pair of you! What do you think you're on?

BAMFORTH: I'm waiting for you, Jock.

SMITH: So go on, Mac. You take a poke at him and where's it get you? You lose your tape, you're in the nick.

MACLEISH: The tape means nothing to me.

SMITH: So all right! You get six months in the nick.

BAMFORTH: What are you waiting for? You're pretty big with the mouth, Jock; let's see you follow it up.

MACLEISH [*raising his fists and moving in on Bamforth*]: You asked for it . . .

SMITH [*restraining Macleish*]: You dim Scotch crone! It's what he wants! He's dying for you to put him one on. Use your loaf! Screw the bomb! Sling in your tape and stick him one on then – if it's going to make you feel any better. Do it then. You put a finger on him

28

now he'll come King's Regs on you so fast your feet won't touch the ground.

MACLEISH [*shrugging Smith away*]: I'll sort him so he never comes King's Regs again. On me or anybody else!

[EVANS *has turned away from the window and all interest is centred on Macleish and Bamforth as the door opens and* MITCHEM *and* JOHNSTONE *enter.*]

MITCHEM: So what's all this in aid of?

JOHNSTONE: Do your jacket up, Bamforth!

BAMFORTH: Must have come undone.

JOHNSTONE: And get your heels together when you speak to me, lad!

BAMFORTH [*coming slowly to attention*]: Corporal.

[*There is an apprehensive pause as* MITCHEM *crosses slowly into the centre of the room.*]

MITCHEM: On your feet! [WHITAKER *rises.*] Get fell in, the lot of you! Move yourselves! [*The members of the patrol, with the exception of Johnstone, fall in in single rank.*] Ted, stand by the door.

JOHNSTONE [*half closes the door and stands on guard*]: Check.

MITCHEM [*he walks slowly along the line of men and turns, flicking open an unbutton breast pocket on Evans's jacket as he walks back.* EVANS *steps one pace out of the ranks, fastens the button, and moves back into line.* MITCHEM *looks along the line of men. There is a long pause before he speaks.*]: Shower! Useless shower! That's all you are. The lot of you. I could have been a regiment of ruddy Nips and I walked through that door. I walked straight in! . . . Squad – shun! Stand at ease. Squad – shun! Stand at ease. Corporal Macleish!

MACLEASH [*steps one pace forward smartly*]: Sarnt!

MITCHEM: I left you in charge.

MACLEISH: Sarnt!

MITCHEM: So what happened?

MACLEISH: I . . . I had occasion to reprimand . . . I'm sorry, Sergeant. I forgot myself for the moment.

MITCHEM [*pause*]: So you're sorry. You forgot yourself. I leave you in charge of the section for ten minutes and the whole organization goes to pot. Ten minutes, Corporal, and you're running a monkey house! [*Pause.* MITCHEM *walks along the line and back.*] You had occasion to reprimand who?

MACLEISH: I . . . I forget now, Sergeant. It was one of the men.

MITCHEM: I didn't think it was a chimpanzee. Who was it?

MACLEISH: It was something that happened in the heat of the moment. I forget now.

MITCHEM: Then you'd better remember. Smartish. Corporal Macleish, who was the man?

MACLEISH: If it's all the same to you, Sergeant, I'd prefer not to say.

MITCHEM: For your information, Macleish, it's not the same to me. Just what do you think this is? Just what? All girls together and no telling tales? You think I'm running a Sunday School outing? 'Please, Miss, it was Jimmie Smith who sat on the tomato sandwiches but I promised not to tell.' [EVANS *laughs.*] Shut up!

MACLEISH: It was a personal matter I'd prefer to handle in my own way.

MITCHEM: Then let me put you straight, Corporal. Right now. Before it's too late. You haven't got no personal matters. Not while you're out with me. While you were settling it in your own way – sorting out your personal matters – you could have had seven men, including yourself, with their tripes on the floor. Remember that. Seven. Including me. And as far as I'm concerned, what happens to me's important. [*Addressing the patrol.*] To look at some of you the army's not gained all that much by his incompetence. But, all the same, I brought you out and I intend to take you back. The lot of you. I'll not stand any more from any one of you who makes it awkward for the rest. I want the man who started all this argument to stand out now. . . . Come on, come on! [*There is a pause.*] All right. Fair enough. Have it how you want. You'll all be on fatigues when we get back to camp.

MACLEISH: You can't punish all the section.

MITCHEM: I can do just what I like, Corporal. I can have your guts for garters if I want.

MACLEISH: It's against all army regulations.

[BAMFORTH *takes one pace forward.*]

MITCHEM [*crossing to face Bamforth*]: Hello! What's this? I was wrong.

30

It was a chimpanzee. As if I hadn't guessed. Private Bamforth, eight-double-seven.

BAMFORTH: Sarnt!

MITCHEM: Coming it on again. Coming it on. It's about time you and me had a few words.

BAMFORTH: Sarnt?

MITCHEM: Now get this, Bamforth. Get it straight. Get it in your head. Since you've been posted out to join this mob it's crossed my mind, a time or two, that you don't like the army.

BAMFORTH: Sarnt.

MITCHEM: It's a mutual feeling, Bamforth. The army's not in love with you. If I had you in my lot in Blighty, lad, you wouldn't last a week. I've met your kind before. I've seen men who'd make a breakfast out of muck like you go in the nick and do their time and come back so that butter wouldn't melt between their crutch. Don't try and come the hard-case stuff with me, son. It doesn't work. I'm up to all them tricks myself. O.K.?

BAMFORTH: Sarnt.

MITCHEM: I've watched you, lad. I've had my eye on you. Ever since you first turned up. I've seen you try and come it on with every junior N.C.O. that's been made up. The barrack-room lawyer. The hard case. You can quote King's Regs from now until the middle of next week. Up to every dodge and skive that's in the book. There's just one thing. It doesn't work with me, 'cause I don't work according to the book. You don't know anything, Bamforth. You don't know anything at all. But if you want to try and come it on with me I'll tell you, here and now, that I can be a bastard. I can be the biggest bastard of them all. And just remember this: I've got three stripes start on you. You're a non-runner, son, I start favourite halfway down the course before the off. You haven't got a chance. So now just go ahead and play it how you want. I'm easy. [*Pause.*] Now get back into line the pair of you. Move! [MACLEISH *and* BAMFORTH *step back into the rank.* MITCHEM *crosses to speak to Bamforth.*] And if you take my tip you'll stay in line. [MITCHEM *steps back to address the patrol.*] Stand at ease! ... Easy ... [*The men relax.*] Now, pay attention – all of you. We've

31

had a sortie round, Corporal Johnstone and myself; I'll try and put you in the picture now before we set off back. The main track is about sixty yards from here through the trees. The way we came – and that's the way we're going back. Round the back of here the undergrowth's so thick it would take a month of Sundays to hack half a mile. There's only one way out and that's where we came in. It's over fifteen miles from here to camp and we're moving off in fifteen minutes' time. We march at five-yard intervals – I don't want any of you closing up. Corporal Johnstone's breaking trail and I'll bring up the rear. There'll be no talking. I've said there'll be a five-yard interval between each man. You'll keep it that way. What goes for closing up goes twice as much for dropping back – I don't want any of you falling out. I've told you once it's fifteen miles, or thereabouts, to base. Due south. The other way – north – and twenty miles as near as we can estimate, the line's been built to keep the Nips at bay. All positions have been consolidated. Which means that all the mobs from round these parts have moved up to the front – or most of them – a few have been withdrawn. There's not a living soul, apart from local wogs, if any, for miles from here. If any one of you gets lost he's on his own. I don't advise it. So you keep it five yards – dead. Anybody any questions?

MACLEISH: Sergeant?

MITCHEM: Yeh?

MACLEISH: Have you any idea which of the mobs have moved up country?

MITCHEM: Only what I heard when we left camp. And they were rumours in the mess. Just about the lot, they reckon. The Fusiliers, two regiments of Jocks, and some artillery. You studying Military History?

MACLEISH: No. I've got . . . It's my brother. He's with the Highland boys.

MITCHEM: I see.

MACLEISH: He's my young brother. We've applied to get his transfer to our mob. It's not come through yet. You've heard they've moved them up already?

MITCHEM: It was just a rumour in the mess . . . Anybody else got any ticks? [*There is a negative murmur from the men.*] That makes a change. Right then, Fifteen minutes and we push off back. Who did first stag?

MACLEISH: Smith and myself, Sergeant.

MITCHEM: You two had better have a break. Bamforth, Evans!

BAMFORTH:
EVANS: } Sarge?

MITCHEM: You're both on guard. All right. The rest of you fall out. [BAMFORTH *and* EVANS *pick up their rifles and cross to windows.* MACLEISH *and* SMITH *cross to form and sit down.* JOHNSTONE *closes door and crosses into room as the two reliefs reach the windows.*]

MITCHEM: Whitaker!

WHITAKER: Sergeant?

MITCHEM: Any joy on the set?

WHITAKER: I got something through about five minutes ago, Sarge. I don't know what it was, though. Too faint to pick it up.

JOHNSTONE [*crossing to join Mitchem and Whitaker*]: You got through to base, did you say, Whitaker?

WHITAKER: No, Corp. I got something through, though. I was telling the Sergeant. I picked up something but I don't know what it was.

JOHNSTONE: How much a week do they pay you for this, lad?

MITCHEM: It's not his fault. The battery's dis. O.K., Sammy. Have another go. Better give it one more try.

WHITAKER [*sitting down at set*]: Right, Sergeant. [*He tunes in the set behind following dialogue.*]

JOHNSTONE: What you reckon, Mitch?

MITCHEM: What's that?

JOHNSTONE: What he got?

MITCHEM: Dunno . . . Suppose it must have been the camp. No one else in this area pushing out signals. With a wonky set he couldn't pick up any of the front-line mobs from here. They're out of range. So it figures that it must have been the camp.

JOHNSTONE: I'd like to put the boot in on the burk who dished us out with a u/s batt. S.O.B., that's all they are, the H.O. men.

MITCHEM: We'll sort that out when we get back.

JOHNSTONE: I'd like to ram his pig-muck battery down his throat that's all. Who was on duty in the battery shop?

MITCHEM: It's no good flapping over that. We'll let him have another go and if nothing comes up we'll pack it in. Push off back. We've got a negative report. It doesn't make a lot of difference.

JOHNSTONE: It could have been something else. It could have been important.

MITCHEM: It isn't. So we can sort it out when we get back.

[JOHNSTONE *and* MITCHEM *turn and listen as* WHITAKER *attempts to make contact.*]

WHITAKER: Blue Patrol to Red Leader . . . Blue Patrol calling Red Leader . . . Are you receiving me . . . are you receiving me . . . Come in, Red Leader, come in Red Leader . . . Over.

[WHITAKER *flicks to 'receive' and tunes in. Sound of interference held behind.* JOHNSTONE *and* MITCHEM *listen for a moment and then turn away.*]

JOHNSTONE: Damn duff equipment! The whole damn issue's duff.

MITCHEM [*takes out a packet of cigarettes and offers one to Johnstone*]: Fag?

JOHNSTONE [*taking the cigarette*]: Ta. [*He takes a box of matches from his pocket, strikes one, offers a light to Mitchem, then lights his own.*]

MITCHEM [*inhales deeply then exhales*]: Thanks.

JOHNSTONE: Time do you reckon we'll get back?

MITCHEM: Tomorrow? 'Bout 1800 hours if we keep it up. Roll on. Roll on, let's get some kip.

JOHNSTONE: If you get the chance. Kit inspection Saturday morning. What's the betting we end up on the square after that? C.O.'s parade.

MITCHEM: Not this boy. I'm going to grab a week-end off, and chuff the expense.

WHITAKER [*pushes the headphones on to the back of his head and turns in his chair*]: Sarge!

MITCHEM [*turns*]: Yeh?

WHITAKER: Coming through again!

[MITCHEM *and* JOHNSTONE *cross to table and listen intently to the set.* WHITAKER *replaces headphones and tunes in.* MACLEISH *and*

SMITH, *who have been talking together on the form, sit up and listen. There is an air of expectancy amongst the patrol. As Whitaker fiddles with the controls the interference increases and dies away. A faint murmur of speech can be heard from the set.*]

WHITAKER: There it is!

MITCHEM: Come on, lad! Let's be having it.

EVANS: Ask the C.O. if he loves me as much as always, Whitto boy!

BAMFORTH: Nobody loves you, you horrible Taff!

JOHNSTONE: Shut up! Pack the talking in!

WHITAKER: I've got it now!

[*The radio bursts into life. The voice of a Japanese radio operator comes through the set clearly.* WHITAKER *turns and looks in bewilderment at Mitchem. These two are the first to realize the implications. There is a slight pause, stemming from surprise, then the patrol reacts with forced humour.*]

BAMFORTH: You've got it, Whitto son, all right. You've got the ruddy Japs.

EVANS: If that's the camp they're having rice for tea and my name's Tojo.

BAMFORTH: Bring on the geisha girls!

MACLEISH: A right ruddy radio operator you've turned out to be, Whitaker. You don't know who's side you're on.

MITCHEM [*leans across and switches off the set*]: Pack the talking in, the lot of you! Right, Whitaker. [WHITAKER, *who is staring in horror at the set, makes no reply.*] Whitaker, I'm talking to you, lad! [WHITAKER *looks up for the first time.*] How strong's the battery? ... Come on, come on!

WHITAKER: It's almost gone. The battery's nearly dead.

MITCHEM: So what's your range at present? ... Whitaker, your range!

WHITAKER [*pulling himself together slightly*]: It must be under fifteen miles. I can't get through to camp. It could be ten. It might be less. [*With the exception of Evans the patrol begins to comprehend.*]

EVANS: Go on, Whitto boy! You're up the creek all over. The Japs are past Jalim Besar. It's twenty miles away at least.

SMITH: We're all up the creek.

BAMFORTH: Stroll on.

JOHNSTONE: Evans! Bamforth! You're supposed to be on guard. Get on your posts!

[EVANS *and* BAMFORTH, *who have turned away from the window during the above dialogue, return to their positions.*]

WHITAKER: It was as clear as a bell! They could be sitting right on top of us!

MACLEISH: Under fifteen miles away! So what's happened to the lads up country?

MITCHEM: Shut up.

MACLEISH: What's happened to the forward boys?

MITCHEM: Shut up.

MACLEISH: I've got my brother posted up out there!

MITCHEM: Shut up! Johnno, check the stens.

JOHNSTONE [*crossing to table where he checks Mitchem's sten and his own*]: Right.

MITCHEM [*crossing to Macleish*]: Now just shut up. It makes no difference now to you, lad, if your mother's kipping with a Jap. O.K. [MACLEISH *is about to burst into reply but changes his mind and sits on form.*] Then just remember that. Now listen. All of you. Evans, Bamforth, don't turn round. I want your eyes out there. You got that, both of you? [BAMFORTH *and* EVANS *nod.*] Then ram a round apiece up your spouts. [BAMFORTH *and* EVANS *release the safety catches on their rifles, withdraw the bolts and slam them home.*] O.K. Now put your safety catches on. [BAMFORTH *and* EVANS *hesitate a moment and then comply.*] O.K. That's fine. That's all we need. No more than that. [*He crosses centre-stage to address the patrol.*] Fred Karno's mob. That's what you are, Fred Karno's mob. There's half of you been shooting off your mouths for days on end on how you'd fix the Japs. To listen to you talk you'd win the ruddy war on bread and jam. You've heard one slimy Nippo on the set and now you're having second thoughts. You make me laugh, that's what you do to me – make me want to laugh. [JOHNSTONE *has now finished his examination of the stens.*] O.K., Johnno?

JOHNSTONE: Both O.K.

MITCHEM [*to the patrol*]: You've heard one Nippo on the set. That

36

might mean anything at all. It might mean that they've broken through, up country, and are pouring down. If that's a fact, then chuff your luck. That's all – just chuff your luck. They might be swarming out there now – like ants. And if they are and I'm with crumbs like you, I'm up the creek myself and that's a fact. [*The patrol murmurs uneasily.*] But all you know so far is that you've heard a Nippo griping on the set. And that could mean that somewhere in this festering heat one lousy bunch of Japs have wriggled in behind our lines – that could be half a dozen men. It could be less than that. It could be half a dozen Joskins like yourselves. Six or seven – five or six – or even two or three poor helpless wet-nurse ginks who, somewhere, close to here, are running round in circles, doing their nuts, because they've heard young Whitto pushing out a signal back to base. If that's the way things are with them, the bloke who's calling out the time for 'em has got my sympathy. I wish him luck. He's up to the short hairs in it like myself and so I wish him luck. [*The confidence of the men has been largely restored – one or two are even amused.*] I'll tell you what we're going to do. We're moving off. Right now. [*Murmur of relief from the men.*] We're going back. It's odds on that they're just a buckshee bunch of Harries like yourselves. All the same, we're not waiting to find out. The orders for the movement back still stand. Evans, Bamforth, you'll stay on guard until the others have got their gear on and are ready to move off back.

[*The men begin to struggle into their webbing equipment.*]

JOHNSTONE: Come on, then! Move yourselves! We've not got time to play about!

MITCHEM: Macleish and Smith! [MACLEISH *and* SMITH *pause in assembling their kit.*] Soon as you've got into your gear, relieve the two on guard and let them get theirs on. [MACLEISH *and* SMITH *nod and return to their task.*] Quick as you can.

JOHNSTONE [*picks up the stens and hands one to Mitchem*]: You want me to lead off back?

MITCHEM [*nods*]: Crack the whip a bit. Set a steady pace. I want to try and do it in one stint.

JOHNSTONE: I'm with you.

BAMFORTH [*unnoticed by the others,* BAMFORTH *suddenly tenses himself and raises his rifle. He flicks off the safety catch and takes aim.*]: Sarge ... Sarge!

MITCHEM [*sensing Bamforth's urgency*]: Hold it, all of you!] *The men are still and silent.*] What's up?

BAMFORTH: I thought I saw a movement down the track ... It's there again!

MITCHEM [*to the patrol*]: Get down! Get out of sight! [*Apart from the two men on guard and* MITCHEM *the members of the patrol stoop below the level of the windows.*] How many of them? Can you see?

BAMFORTH [*lowers his rifle*]: No. Out of sight again. Behind the trees. Heading this way.

[MITCHEM, *his head down below window level, moves across the hut to join Bamforth at the window.* JOHNSTONE *moves across to join Evans.*]

MITCHEM: Which way they coming from?

BAMFORTH [*pointing*]: Along the track. Down there. 'Bout fifty yards.

MITCHEM: Evans?

EVANS: Can't see a ruddy thing from here, Sarge. Not as far as that.

JOHNSTONE: There's a clump of blasted bushes in the way.

MITCHEM: Were they Japs?

BAMFORTH: Might have been anything. Only had a glimpse.

MITCHEM: Are you sure, Bamforth?

BAMFORTH: Meaning what?

MITCHEM: You saw anything at all, lad?

BAMFORTH: You think I'm going round the bend!

MITCHEM: All right. We'll take your word for it. If there is anyone down there they should come into sight again just by that bit of ...

BAMFORTH [*nudges Mitchem and points again*]: A Jap!

MITCHEM: I've got him. On his own. [*Turns slightly from window*] Now keep still, all of you. This one's on his tod. Could be a scout. He hasn't spotted this place up to press. Got him, Johnno?

JOHNSTONE: Can't see anything for this ruddy bush. Whereabouts?

MITCHEM: Just less than fifty yards. Straight ahead ... Got him, have you?

JOHNSTONE: Not yet. What do you think he's on?

BAMFORTH: He's . . . He's looking round for something. In the grass. Looking for something . . . Bending down.

JOHNSTONE: Think he's found the trail, Mitch? Up to here?

MITCHEM: Looks like that. Found something by the way he's carrying on.

[BAMFORTH *bursts into laughter.*]

MITCHEM: Shut up!

BAMFORTH: Found the trail! He's found the trail all right! He's found a place to have a crafty smoke.

EVANS: He's what, Bammo?

BAMFORTH: Having a drag. He's lighting up a fag. Well, the crafty old Nip. The skiving get. Caught red-handed. Nip down and ask him for a puff, Taff.

MITCHEM: Of all the rotten luck. He would choose this place. We'll wait and see'f he pushes off . . . [BAMFORTH *slowly raises his rifle and takes careful aim.* MITCHEM *swings round and knocks the rifle out of aiming position.*] I said no noise!

BAMFORTH: I had him right between the cheeks! I couldn't miss! He's on his tod!

MITCHEM: What gives you that idea? Do you think they march off by the dozen for a sly swallow?

JOHNSTONE: What's happening?

BAMFORTH: He's up. He's standing up and nicking out the nub. He's going back. The way he came . . . Stopped . . . Turning round . . . He's coming back. He's found the track up here. He's coming up.

MITCHEM: Move it then, the rest of you. Let's have you over by the wall! And bring your gear.

[MACLEISH, WHITAKER, *and* SMITH *pick up their rifles and the kit and scurry across to the rear wall of the hut.*]

MITCHEM [*peering round window*]: Bamforth, Evans, down on deck! [BAMFORTH *and* EVANS *drop below window level.*] And stay there all of you. There's just a chance he might not come inside. In case he does – Johnno . . . [MITCHEM *indicates the door.* JOHNSTONE *nods and sidles across to stand by the door.* MITCHEM *peers round window.*] If he should come in – you grab. Without a sound. I'll cover the outside

39

in case. Still coming up . . . Close to the wall as you can. He might not see us yet.

WHITAKER [*notices the radio which is still standing on the table*]: Sarge! The set!

MITCHEM: Oh God, lad! Get it! Quick! [WHITAKER *moves as if to cross to table, but changes his mind and hugs the wall in terror.*] Get the set! [*Whitaker is still afraid to move. Smith is about to fetch the radio when we hear the sound of feet on the wooden veranda.*] Too late!

[*The members of the patrol squeeze up against the wall as* MITCHEM *edges away from the window out of sight.* JOHNSTONE *tenses himself. The* JAPANESE SOLDIER *can be heard clattering on the veranda for several seconds before he appears at the left-hand window. He peers into the room but fails to see the patrol and is just about to turn away when he notices the radio on the table. He stares at it for a short while and then moves out of sight as he crosses along the veranda towards the door. A further short pause.* JOHNSTONE *raises his hands in readiness. The door opens and the* JAPANESE SOLDIER *enters. As he steps into the room* JOHNSTONE *lunges forward and grabs the Japanese, putting an arm round his throat and his free hand over the soldier's mouth.* MITCHEM, *holding the sten at his hip, darts out of the door and covers the jungle from the veranda.* JOHNSTONE *and the* PRISONER *struggle in the room.*]

JOHNSTONE: Come on then, one of you! Get him! Quick! . . . Evans! Do for him! [EVANS *crosses and raises his rifle, releasing the safety catch.*] No, you burk! You want to do for me as well? Come on, lad! Use your bayonet! In his guts! You'll have to give it hump. [EVANS *unsheaths his bayonet and approaches the struggling figures.*] Sharp then, lad! Come on! Come on! You want it in between his ribs. [EVANS *raises the bayonet to stab the Prisoner, who squirms in terror.*] Not that way, lad! You'll only bust a bone. Feel for it first, then ram it in. Now, come on, quick! [*Evans places his bayonet point on the chest of the Prisoner, who has now stopped struggling and is cringing in the grip of* JOHNSTONE.] Come on! Come on! I can't hold on to him forever! Will you ram it in!

EVANS [*steps back*]: I . . . I can't do it, Corp.

JOHNSTONE: Stick it in! Don't stand there tossing up the odds! Just close your eyes and whoof it in!

EVANS: I can't! I can't! Corp, I can't.

JOHNSTONE: Macleish!

MACLEISH: Not me!

JOHNSTONE: Smith! Take the bayonet! Don't stand there gawping. Do the job!

SMITH: For God's sake do it, Taff. Put the poor bastard out of his misery.

EVANS [proffering the bayonet to Smith]: You!

BAMFORTH [crossing and snatching the bayonet from Evans]: Here. Give me hold. It's only the same as carving up a pig. Hold him still.

[BAMFORTH raises the bayonet and is about to thrust it into the chest of the Prisoner as MITCHEM enters, closing the door behind him.]

MITCHEM: Bamforth! Hold it!

BAMFORTH [hesitates, then moves away]: I'm only doing what I'm told.

MITCHEM: Just hold it, that's all. I want this one alive. You'll have your chance before we've done. You can count on that. So pack in all this greyhound with a bunny lark. He's not the only one; you'll have your chance. How is he, Johnno? Is he going to do his nut?

JOHNSTONE: Scared stiff. He's going up the wall. I've had enough of him – he stinks of garlic and wog grub. He won't try anything – I wouldn't trust his mouth.

MITCHEM: Hold him for a sec. [MITCHEM crosses close up to the Prisoner.] You speakee English? Understand? Compronney? Eh? Eh? You speakee English talk? Trust me to cop a raving lunatic. You! I want no noise, see? Understand? No noise! Quiet. [MITCHEM points to his mouth and shakes his head.] No speakee! Keep your trap shut, eh? Now get this, Tojo. Understand. You make so much as a mutter and I'll let Jack the Ripper have a go at you. [MITCHEM indicates Bamforth, who is still holding the bayonet. The PRISONER cringes in Johnstone's grip.] O.K.? [MITCHEM points again to his mouth and the PRISONER nods vigorously.] Good. One murmur, Jap, and Laughing Boy will slit your guts up to your ears. Universal talk. I think I'm getting through to him at last, Bamforth!

BAMFORTH [crossing to Mitchem]: Sarge?

MITCHEM: Put the carving knife away before he dies on us of fright.

BAMFORTH [*turns the bayonet over in his hand and makes a quick, playful gesture with the weapon towards the Prisoner's throat. The* PRISONER *struggles again in Johnstone's arms*]: Boo!

MITCHEM: Bamforth! Jack it in! I said put the cutlery away.

BAMFORTH: All right! [*He crosses and returns the bayonet to* EVANS *who replaces it in the sheath. The* PRISONER *calms down.*] Thanks, Taff.

MITCHEM: Right, Johnno. He'll behave himself. He'll be a good lad. Put him down.

[JOHNSTONE *pushes the Prisoner away.* MITCHEM *gestures with the sten and the* PRISONER'S *arms fly up above his head. The Prisoner is a small, round, pathetic, and almost comic character, armed to the teeth in a Gilbertian fashion; a revolver in a leather holster is slung round his chest and a string of hand grenades swings from his waist. A long two-edged bayonet hangs from his belt. He wears a drab, ill-fitting uniform, peaked cap, and a white silk muffler is tied round his throat. As the Prisoner stands alone and afraid in the centre of the hut the patrol cluster round to examine him.*]

EVANS: He looks as if he's going to fight the war himself.

MACLEISH: He's not exactly what you'd call a handsome bloke.

MITCHEM: All right, get back. What do you want, Jock? A blonde? I'll fix it so it's Rita Hayworth walks in next. Move it! Back!

[*The members of the patrol cross over to the left as* MITCHEM *ushers the Prisoner towards the right-hand wall.*]

JOHNSTONE: Come on then! Move yourselves! He doesn't put the wind up you lot now? You're round him like a lot of lambs that's had their first taste of milk. Two minutes since you wouldn't touch him with a barge pole. None of you!

MITCHEM: Bamforth! Take the armoury away.

BAMFORTH [*crosses to the Prisoner, who cringes away as he approaches*]: Stand still, you nig! Unless you want the boot! [BAMFORTH *proceeds to remove the weapons from the Prisoner, also checking him for any further arms.*]

JOHNSTONE: A right lot I've got landed with! Not one of you had the guts to give me a hand.

MACLEISH: You weren't in need of help. You cannot order men to put a bayonet in an unarmed prisoner.

JOHNSTONE: What do you think they dish you out with bayonets for? Just opening tins of soup?

MACLEISH: They're not to put in prisoners of war!

JOHNSTONE: You know what you can do with yours. You wouldn't know which end is which!

MACLEISH: If the need should arise I'll use a bayonet with the next. But I've no intention of using one on any man who can't defend himself.

JOHNSTONE: You burk!

MACLEISH: He was a prisoner of war!

JOHNSTONE: Prisoner my crutch!

MACLEISH: There such a thing as the Geneva Convention!

JOHNSTONE: He's carting more cannon than the Woolwich Arsenal! If he'd have pulled the pin on one of them grenades we'd all of us been up the shoot! You think that he'd have second thoughts before he put the mockers on the lot of us?

BAMFORTH [places the Prisoner's arms on the table]: That's about the lot.

MITCHEM: Which of you men's supposed to be on guard? The war's not won because you've copped a Nip!

EVANS: I was, Sarge.

MITCHEM: Get on your post and stay there, lad. Who else?

BAMFORTH: Me.

MITCHEM: I've got another job for you. Anybody else that's not done stag so far?

WHITAKER: I haven't been on guard yet, Sarge. I was on the set.

MITCHEM: Then get on now. Take Bamforth's number. [EVANS and WHITAKER pick up their rifles and cross to the windows.] Bamforth!

BAMFORTH: Sarge?

MITCHEM [offering his sten to Bamforth]: Here. Cop on for this. You're looking after Tojo here. I think he fancies you. If he tries to come it on he gets it through the head. No messing. He's in your charge. Look after him.

BAMFORTH [shakes his head, refusing the sten]: Like he was my only chick. [BAMFORTH picks up the Prisoner's bayonet from the table.] I'll settle for this. [*He crosses towards the Prisoner.*] Down, Shorthouse. [*He motions the Prisoner to sit on the form.*] Put your hands up on your head. [*The* PRISONER *looks at Bamforth in bewilderment.*] I said, get your hands up on your head! Like this! See! Flingers on the blonce! All-light? [BAMFORTH *demonstrates and the Prisoner complies.* BAM-FORTH *is delighted.*] Hey, Taff! See that, did you? He did it like I said! Flingers up on blonce. I only talk the lingo natural!

EVANS [*turning at window*]: I always knew you were an Oriental creep at heart, man!

BAMFORTH: You've not seen nothing yet – get this. [*To the Prisoner.*] Allee-lightee. Flingers up to touch the loof. Come on, come on! Touch the loof, you Asiatic glet! [BAMFORTH *raises the bayonet and the* PRISONER *cringes away.*] He's a rotten ignoramus.

MITCHEM: All right, that'll do. Pack it in. Now listen, all of you. We're taking this boy back to camp with us. I want to get him there in one piece.

JOHNSTONE: It's a bit dodgy, isn't it, Mitch?

MITCHEM: Happen.

JOHNSTONE: It's going to be a dodgy number as it is. You don't know how many more of them there are out there.

MITCHEM: Not yet.

JOHNSTONE: They could be coming down in strength.

MITCHEM: They might.

JOHNSTONE: And if they are we're up the creek all right. We've got enough on getting this lot back. They've no experience. We'll have to belt it like the clappers out of hell. We can't afford to hang about.

MITCHEM: We'll shift.

JOHNSTONE: But if we're going to cart a prisoner along as well . . .

MITCHEM: He'll go the pace. I'll see to that.

JOHNSTONE: You're in charge.

MITCHEM: That's right. Corporal Macleish! Smith!

MACLEISH: Sergeant?

SMITH: Sarge?

MITCHEM: I've got a job for you two. Outside. [MACLEISH *and* SMITH *exchange glances.*] I want the pair of you to nip down as

far as the main track. Look for any signs of any more of them.
O.K.?

MACLEISH: You want us to go down now, Sarge?

MITCHEM: Straight away. If the coast's clear we want to belt off back.
Smartish.

MACLEISH: Right.

MITCHEM: Take it steady – careful – but don't make a meal out of it.
The sooner we can make a start from here the better.

[MACLEISH and SMITH strap on their ammunition pouches.]

MACLEISH: Supposing we should . . . make contact?

MITCHEM: Don't. Not if you can help it. If you see anything that
moves – turn back. Mac, you'd better take a sten. Take mine.
[MACLEISH crosses and takes sten and a couple of clips of ammunition
from Mitchem, SMITH unsheaths his bayonet and clips it on his rifle.]
Come on. [MITCHEM, MACLEISH, and SMITH cross to the door.]
What's it like out, Evans?

EVANS: Quiet. Quiet as a grave.

WHITAKER: Nothing this side, Sarge.

MITCHEM: Cover them as far as you can down the track. [EVANS
and WHITAKER nod. MITCHEM opens door slowly and ushers SMITH
and MACLEISH on to the veranda.] Off you go.

EVANS: So long, Smudger, Jock.

MITCHEM [closes door and crosses to where Bamforth is guarding the
Prisoner]: How's he behaving himself?

BAMFORTH [fingering the bayonet]: All right. He hasn't got much
choice.

MITCHEM [to the Prisoner]: You listen to me. Understand? You come
with us. We take you back. We take you back with us. Oh, blimey
. . . Look . . . Bamforth.

BAMFORTH: Yeh?

MITCHEM: Tell him he can drop his hands. He isn't going to run
away.

BAMFORTH: Hey, Tojo! Flingers off blonce. Flingers off blonce! [The
PRISONER raises his hands in the air.] Not that, you nit! Here, that's
not bad though, is it? He's coming on. He knows his flingers
already. Good old Tojo! [The PRISONER smiles.] Now let them

dlop. Dlop, see! Down! [BAMFORTH *demonstrates and the* PRISONER *slowly drops his hands.*] He picks up quick. He's a glutton for knowledge.

MITCHEM [*speaks slowly and carefully*] : You – come – with – us! Back! We – take – you – back! [*The Prisoner is mystified.*] Back to camp! [MITCHEM *turns away.*] What's the use ... [MITCHEM *crosses to table.*]

BAMFORTH: I'll work on him. I'll chat him up a bit.

JOHNSTONE: We should have done him first time off.

MITCHEM: I'm giving the orders!

BAMFORTH: Flingers on blonce. [*The* PRISONER *complies happily.*] Dlop flingers. [*Again the* PRISONER *obeys.*] Get that! He dlops them like a two-year-old!

JOHNSTONE: Just keep him quiet, Bamforth, that's all. We don't want any of the funny patter!

BAMFORTH: I'm teaching him to talk!

JOHNSTONE: Well don't! Mitch, we've got fifteen miles to slog it back. We've got no set. We know the Japs are coming through – so someone's waiting for a report – and quick. We can't drag him along – suppose he tries to come it on? One shout from him with any of his boys around we're in the cart. The lot of us.

MITCHEM: So what do you suggest?

JOHNSTONE: Get rid of him. Right now. You going soft?

MITCHEM: And if we do? You want to make out the report when we get back?

JOHNSTONE: Report! You want to make out a report! Because we do a Jap? We whip him out and knock him off, that's all. We can't take prisoners. We're out to do a job.

MITCHEM: Reports on him don't bother me. And if I've got to do for him – I will. I'll knock him off myself. You think I'm stuffing my nut worrying about a Jap? One Jap? I've got six men. They're my responsibility. But more than that, and like you say, I've got a job to do. So all right. So I'll do it. Now you tell me what's going on out there? [MITCHEM *indicates the window.*] Just tell me how many Nips have broken through and where they are right now. You want to wait and count them for yourself?

JOHNSTONE: I want to slog it back!

MITCHEM: All right. That's what we're going to do. With him. [*Points to the Prisoner.*] With Tojo there. Because if anybody knows the strength of Nips behind our lines it's him. So far on this outing out it's been the biggest muck-up in the history of the British Army, and that's saying a lot. We've wandered round, the set's packed in, we've no idea what's going on and if there ever was an organized shambles – my God, this is it. Now things have changed. We've copped on to a lad who's going to make this detail worth its while. If I can get him back to camp what they'll get out of him could do more good than you if you should serve a score and one. So he's important for what he knows. And I'll leave any man on this patrol behind – including you – before I'll say good-bye to him. Going soft? Do you think I give a twopenny damn about his life? It's what he knows.

JOHNSTONE: Suppose he comes the ab-dabs on the way?

MITCHEM: He won't.

JOHNSTONE: But if he does? He only needs to start playing it up at the wrong time. He only wants to start coming it on when we're close to his muckers.

MITCHEM: I've said he won't.

JOHNSTONE: What if he does?

[MITCHEM *and* JOHNSTONE *glance across at the Prisoner.*]

MITCHEM: I'll put the bayonet in his guts myself. [*Pause*] You'd better check these Jap grenades. Might come in handy.

[MITCHEM *and* JOHNSTONE *turn to table to check the grenades. The Prisoner's hand goes up to his breast pocket.* BAMFORTH *raises the bayonet threateningly.*]

BAMFORTH: Watch it, Tojo boy! Just watch your step! I'll have it in as soon as look at you!

MITCHEM [*glancing round*]: What's up with him?

BAMFORTH: Going for his pocket.

[*The* PRISONER *gestures towards his pocket.*]

MITCHEM: All right. See what he wants.

BAMFORTH [*still threatening with the bayonet, he opens the Prisoner's breast pocket and takes out a cheap leather wallet*]: It's his wallet.

JOHNSTONE: Sling it out the window.

MITCHEM: Let him have it. Check it first.

[BAMFORTH *briefly inspects the interior of the wallet.*]

JOHNSTONE: You're going to let him have it?

MITCHEM: It costs us nothing. No point in getting him niggly before we start.

BAMFORTH: Looks all right, Sarge.

MITCHEM: Give it him.

[BAMFORTH *hands the wallet to the Prisoner, who opens it, extracts a couple of photographs, and hands one to Bamforth.*]

BAMFORTH: It's a photo! It's a picture of a Nippo bint! [*The* PRISONER *points proudly to himself.*] Who's this, then, eh? You got wife? Your missis? [*The* PRISONER *points again to himself.*] It's his old woman! Very good. Plenty of humpy. Japanese girl very good, eh? Good old Tojo! She's a bit short in the pins, that's all. But very nice. I wouldn't mind a crack at her myself. [*The* PRISONER *passes another photograph to Bamforth.*] Here! Get this! Nippo snappers, Sarge. Two Jap kids. Couple of chicos. You got two chicos, eh? [*The* PRISONER *does not understand. Bamforth points to photograph and holds up two fingers.*] Two! See? You got two kids. [*The* PRISONER *shakes his head and holds up three fingers.*] Three? No, you stupid raving imbecile! Two! [BAMFORTH *points again to the photograph.*] One and one's two! Dinky-doo-number two! [*The* PRISONER *holds up his hands to indicate a baby.*] What another? Another one as well! Well, you crafty old devil! You're a bit fond of it, aren't you? You're a rotten old sex maniac, you are. You're as bad as Smudge. [BAMFORTH *returns the photographs to the* PRISONER, *who replaces them carefully in his wallet and returns it to his pocket.*] Let's see if you still know your lessons. Flingers up on blonce! [*The* PRISONER *complies.*] Dlop flingers! [*Again the* PRISONER *is happy to obey.*] Stroll on! See that? He got it right both times! He's almost human this one is!

MITCHEM: All right, Bamforth, jack it in!

JOHNSTONE: We should have done him when he first turned up.

MITCHEM [*crossing to Evans*]: Where have them two got to?

EVANS: No sign yet, Sarge.

[MITCHEM *peers out of window.* BAMFORTH *takes out a packet of cigarettes and puts one in his mouth. He replaces the packet in his pocket and feels for a box of matches as his glance falls on the Prisoner, who is looking up at him.* BAMFORTH *hesitates, then transfers the cigarette from his own mouth to the Prisoner's. He takes out another cigarette for himself.* JOHNSTONE *rises and crosses to Bamforth.* BAMFORTH *is still looking for a match as* JOHNSTONE *takes out a box, strikes one, and offers Bamforth a light.*]

BAMFORTH: Ta. [JOHNSTONE *holds out the match for the Prisoner. As the* PRISONER *leans across to get a light,* JOHNSTONE *knocks the cigarette from his mouth with the back of his hand.*] What's that in aid of?

JOHNSTONE: He gets permission first!

BAMFORTH: I gave him it!

JOHNSTONE: Since when have you been calling out the time!

BAMFORTH: I don't ask you before I give a bloke a fag?

JOHNSTONE: This one you do!

BAMFORTH: Who says?

JOHNSTONE: I do, lad! [*Making a sudden grab for the Prisoner and attempting to tear open his breast pocket.*] I'll fix his photos for the Herb as well!

MITCHEM [*turns*]: Corporal Johnstone!

BAMFORTH [*drops the bayonet and clutches Johnstone by his jacket lapels. He brings his knee up in Johnstone's groin and, as* JOHNSTONE *doubles forward,* BAMFORTH *cracks his forehead across the bridge of Johnstone's nose.*]: Have that!

MITCHEM [*crossing towards the fight*]: Bamforth!
[BAMFORTH, *unheeding, strikes Johnstone in the stomach and pushes him to the floor.*]

JOHNSTONE [*pulling himself to his feet*]: All right. You've done it this time, Bamforth! You've shot your load. As sure as God you'll get three years for that.

BAMFORTH [*picks up bayonet*]: You try and make it stick.

MITCHEM: You're on a charge, Bamforth. You're under open arrest.

BAMFORTH: He started it!

MITCHEM: Tell that to the c.o.

EVANS [*raising his rifle*]: Sarge! There's someone coming up the track!

49

MITCHEM [*crosses to window*]: Whereabouts?

EVANS: Just coming through the trees.

[JOHNSTONE *picks up his sten and crosses to join Whitaker.*]

MITCHEM: It's all right. It's Macleish and Smith. Cover them up the track.

JOHNSTONE [*aiming the sten*]: I've got them.

EVANS: Looks as if they're in a hurry over something.

[*A pause before we hear* MACLEISH *and* SMITH *clatter up on to the veranda.* MITCHEM *opens the door and they enter the room. They lean against the wall exhausted.*]

MITCHEM: Anybody after you? [MACLEISH *shakes his head.*] What's up then?

EVANS: What's the hurry, Smudger boy? You look as if you've had the whole of the Japanese army on your tail.

SMITH [*out of breath*]: We have . . . Near enough.

MITCHEM: Sit down a tick. [SMITH *and* MACLEISH *cross the table and sit down.* MITCHEM *crosses to join them.*] Now, come on – give. Let's be having it.

MACLEISH [*regaining his breath*]: They've broken through. In strength. There's hundreds of them moving down the main trail back.

MITCHEM: Go on.

SMITH: They must have come through our defence lines like a dose of salts. They're pouring down. Happy as a lot of sand boys. Not a mark on any one of them. Up front the whole damn shoot's collapsed.

MITCHEM: You weren't spotted?

MACLEISH [*shakes his head*]: They're not even looking for anybody. They seem to know they've got this area to themselves. Smudge and myself got down in the long grass. They've got no scouts out. Nothing. Just strolling down the trail as if they owned the jungle . . .

MITCHEM: Do you think they'll find this place?

MACLEISH: Not yet awhile. We watched about a company march past. There was a break then in the file. We managed to cover up the entrance of the trail up here.

SMITH: We stuffed it up with bits of branch and stuff.

MITCHEM: Good.

MACLEISH: The next batch came along as we were finishing. We patched up what we could and scooted back.

JOHNSTONE: So what happens now?

MITCHEM: It's put the kybosh on the journey back. We can't move out of here just yet, and that's a certainty.

MACLEISH: You never saw so many Japs. There must be at least a thousand of them now between ourselves and base. We're right behind their forward lines.

MITCHEM [crosses down-stage and turns]: Let's say, for now, they march without a stop. That brings them close up on the camp before tomorrow night. If they've got stuff up in the air to back them up – and if they don't know back at base they've broken through – the base mob gets wiped up.

MACLEISH: But they'll know by now the Japs are through.

MITCHEM: We can't count on that.

JOHNSTONE: If the main road's free, they'll have heavy transport loads of Nips chugging down before tomorrow.

MITCHEM: Let's hope the Engineers have sewn that up. They'll have it mined at least. No, this is the back way in. Cross-country – and it's hard graft cutting trail – they'll have to do the lot on foot.

JOHNSTONE: So?

MITCHEM: So that means we can put the blocks on them. We get there first.

JOHNSTONE: You think the Japs are going to open ranks and let us pass?

MITCHEM: What's the time now? [He glances at his watch.] It'll be dark in just over an hour. We might make it then.

JOHNSTONE: And so you think we stand a chance at creeping through a regiment of ruddy Nips!

MITCHEM: What's your suggestion?

JOHNSTONE: We haven't got a chance.

MITCHEM: We've got no choice. We might make it in the dark and in that shrub. They'll be blundering about themselves. At least we know the way – we've done it coming up. It's all new ground to them. We might creep through.

JOHNSTONE [indicating the Prisoner]: What? With him in tow?

MITCHEM [*glancing across at the Prisoner*]: No . . . We're ditching him. Whitaker!

WHITAKER [*turning at window*]: Sarge?

MITCHEM [*indicating set*]: Come on. You'd better give it one more try.

WHITAKER: I don't think it'll do any good, Sarge. The battery's nigh on stone dead.

MITCHEM: Try it, lad! Don't argue. Relieve him, Smith.

[SMITH *crosses to take Whitaker's place at the window as* WHITAKER *crosses to table and sits at set. He switches on to 'transmit' and pauses.*]

MITCHEM: Come on, lad! Get on with it! We haven't time to mess about.

WHITAKER [*turning in his chair to speak to Mitchem*]: If there are any Japs near here switched to receive they'll get a fix on us.

MITCHEM: That can't be helped. Come on, come on!

WHITAKER [*putting on headphones and tuning in*]: Blue Patrol to Red Leader . . . Blue Patrol to Red Leader . . . Are you receiving me . . . Are you receiving me . . . Come in Red Leader . . . Come in Red Leader . . . Over . . . [WHITAKER *switches to 'receive' and tunes in. We hear the crackle of interference.*] Nothing yet . . .

MITCHEM: Come in, Sammy son, come in . . .

WHITAKER [*adjusting tuning dial*]: There's something here . . . [*The interference dies away and we hear the voice of the Japanese* RADIO OPERATOR *as before.*] It's the Jap transmitting. Same as before.

MITCHEM: Get off the ruddy line, you Nip!

[*The voice continues in Japanese for a few seconds and then stops. It continues in taunting broken English.*]

OPERATOR: Johnee! . . . Johnee! . . . British Johnee! We – you – come – to – get . . . We – you – come – to – get.

[WHITAKER *starts up in fear and* MITCHEM *pushes him back into his chair. The patrol turn and look at the Prisoner. The* PRISONER, *noting that all attention is centred on himself, and feeling that he is expected to entertain the patrol, raises his hands in the air and slowly places them on his head. He smiles round blandly in search of approbation.*]

CURTAIN

Time : Thirty minutes later.

[*As the curtain rises we discover* BAMFORTH, EVANS, *and* JOHN-
STONE *asleep on the ground by the wall, left.* MACLEISH *is guarding the Prisoner, who is still sitting on the form where we left
him.* SMITH *and* WHITAKER *are standing at the rear windows.*
MITCHEM *is seated at the table cleaning his sten. A bird sings out in
the jungle and* WHITAKER *starts and raises his rifle. He realizes the
cause of his fears and glances round the room in embarrassment. The
other occupants, however, have not noticed this lapse on the part of
Whitaker.* MITCHEM *places his sten on the table and crosses to
Smith.*]

MITCHEM: All O.K., Smudge?

SMITH: All O.K.

MITCHEM: Sammy?

WHITAKER: Nothing to report here, Sarnt. What time is it now?

MITCHEM [*glances at his watch*]: 'Bout quarter past. [*He returns to his
task at the table.*]

SMITH: Why don't you buy a watch?

WHITAKER: I had one, Smudger. Bought one down the town once.
When I had a week-end off one time. Twenty-eight bucks it was.
A good one.

SMITH: Twenty-eight! For a watch? They saw you coming, and no
mistake.

WHITAKER: No, man, it was a good one, I tell you. Smasher. Told
you the date and what day it was and all that. Little red jewels for
numbers and a sort of little moon came up to tell you when it's
night.

SMITH: You can see when it's night. It gets dark.

WHITAKER: Aye, but it was a smashing watch, Smudge. You can't
get watches like that one was in Blighty. There was a bloke in the

NAAFI offered me forty bucks for it once. Forty bucks and a sort of Siamese ring he was wearing.

SMITH: You took it?

WHITAKER: I turned it down.

SMITH: What for?

WHITAKER: I'm not a fool altogether. You wouldn't get another watch like that. I was going to give it to the old man as a present when we get back home. I wouldn't have minded the ring though. That was a beauty. Peruvian gold.

SMITH: I thought you said it was Siamese?

WHITAKER: It was. It had a kind of Siamese bint on the front. Doing a sort of dance with her knees bent in front of a temple – her hands sticking up in the air.

SMITH: So where is it?

WHITAKER: It wouldn't come off his finger.

SMITH: I mean the watch.

WHITAKER: I wasn't going to swop the watch for that, boy. I've got more sense than that. I could have flogged it for a fortune back in Blighty – if I hadn't have been going to give it to the old man for his present.

SMITH: So where is it then?

WHITAKER: I lost it. Well, it got knocked off. It was half-inched back in camp. I left it in the ablutions one morning while I went off to the latrine. I wasn't gone above two minutes – it was about the time they were giving us fruit salad twice a day and dehydrated spuds. When I came back it was gone. Two minutes at the most. My tooth-paste was gone as well. That was the most expensive trot to the lav that I ever had, I know that. Boy, there's some thieving rascals round that camp.

SMITH: You should have reported it to the RSM. Had a personal kit inspection.

WHITAKER: Ah, what would have been the use? I wouldn't have got it back. If anybody pinched a watch like that he wouldn't leave it lying around in his locker, man. He'd want his head looking at. I've never bought another one since then. I haven't had the heart for it. What time did you say it was, Sarnt?

MITCHEM: I've just told you.

WHITAKER: I forgot.

MITCHEM: Quarter past.

WHITAKER: Roll on. Roll on my relief and let me get my head down. Sergeant Mitchem?

MITCHEM: What is it? What's up now?

WHITAKER: What time we setting off?

MITCHEM: I'll tell you. When it's time to move. We won't leave you behind. Don't worry. No need to flap.

[WHITAKER, *who has been talking to take his mind off other things, relapses into silence.*]

MITCHEM [*takes out his water bottle and has a drink. He glances across at the Prisoner and hands the water bottle to Macleish*]: Here, Jock. See'f Noisy Harry wants a gob.

MACLEISH: Right, Sarge. [MACLEISH *offers the water bottle to the Prisoner who accepts it gratefully. The* PRISONER *takes two pulls at the bottle, wipes the mouth, recorks it, and hands it back to Macleish who, in turn, returns it to Mitchem.*] Your bottle.

MITCHEM [*glances up from cleaning the sten as* MACLEISH *places the water bottle on the table*]: Right. Thanks.

MACLEISH [*anxious to start a conversation*]: He doesn't seem a bad sort of bloke.

MITCHEM: Who? Him?

MACLEISH: I suppose there's good and bad wherever you look. I mean, he's quiet enough.

MITCHEM: What did you expect?

MACLEISH: Oh, I don't know . . . You hear these tales. I suppose it is all over? Up country, I mean?

MITCHEM: You saw them coming through, lad.

MACLEISH: Aye. Only I was wondering if they'd taken many prisoners themselves. The Japs, I mean.

MITCHEM: Search me.

MACLEISH: It seems to me . . . I've been thinking it over, like, in my mind. And I was thinking, at the little time it's taken them to get down here – as far as this – they couldn't have had a lot of resistance.

I mean, do you think it's possible there's been a sort of general jacking in from our lads?

MITCHEM: Happen. I don't know.

MACLEISH: I mean, if there'd been anything like a scrap at all they'd still be at it now, if you see what I mean.

MITCHEM: It follows. They might be still at it, for all we know. Mopping up. We don't know how much of the front still stands – if any. It could be just a section of the line packed in.

MACLEISH: I was wondering about Donald – that's my brother.

MITCHEM: Yeh?

MACLEISH: Well, if you work on the assumption that it's all over – that they've come straight through . . .

MITCHEM: It doesn't do to count on 'ifs' in this lark.

MACLEISH: No. But if they have it's likely that they've copped a lot of prisoners, the Japs. That stands to reason.

MITCHEM: That's fair enough.

MACLEISH: So it's possible my brother is a P.O.W. already.

MITCHEM: There's a chance of that.

MACLEISH: You hear so many stories – you know, on how the Japs treat P.O.W.s.

MITCHEM: Pretty rough, they reckon.

MACLEISH: I'm not so sure. You hear all kinds of things. As if they're almost . . . animals. But this bloke seems a decent sort of bloke.

MITCHEM: It's hard to tell.

MACLEISH: I mean, he's a family man himself.

MITCHEM: So what? Is that supposed to make a difference?

MACLEISH: He's human at least.

MITCHEM: What do you want for your money? Dracula? Look, son, forget the home and family bull. You put a bloke in uniform and push him overseas and he's a different bloke to what he was before. I've watched it happen scores of times.

MACLEISH: But if a bloke's got a wife and family himself . . .

MITCHEM: You get a bloke between your sights and stop to wonder if he's got a family, Jock, your family's not got you. There's half of them got families and most of them are nigs like us who don't know

why we're here or what it's all in aid of. It's not your worry that.
You're not paid to think.

MACLEISH: I used to wonder ... Worried me a lot ... I've often
wondered, if it came to the push, was it inside me to kill a man.

MITCHEM: It's inside all of us. That's the trouble. Just needs fetching
out, and some need more to bring it out than others.

MACLEISH: You know – when we got this one – when he first came
in – I couldn't do it. I just couldn't move. I don't know now
whether I'm sorry or I'm glad.

MITCHEM: You'll do it if it's necessary.

MACLEISH: I'm not worried, mind. I mean, I'm not afraid or anything like that. At least, I don't think I'm afraid no more than
anybody else. I think if it was outside it would be different. The way
you look at things, I mean. If it was him or me. Something moving
about in the trees – something you can put a bullet in and not have
to ... have to look into its eyes.

MITCHEM: I've told you once – you think too much. Outside or else
in here – what's the difference?

MACLEISH: Outside he's got a fighting chance.

MITCHEM: Don't come that. It's not a game of darts. You can't wipe
the board clean and start all over again. Mugs away. The mugs have
had it. There are far too many mugs about. We're all mugs, and
I'll tell you why. I'll tell you what's the trouble with this world,
Jock – bints.

MACLEISH [amused]: Go on!

MITCHEM: It's right. Straight up. They cause more upset than
enough. Half the scrapping in this world is over judies. There's half
the blokes out here now who'd be sitting back in Blighty still with
wangled home postings if it wasn't for a bint. It's bints who go a
bundle over uniforms. You take a bloke – an ordinary bloke who
gets called up. He doesn't want to go. He doesn't want to come out
here, or if he does he's round the bend. Then, one day, this poor
Charlie winds up with a bird – it happens to us all in the end. A
blonde bird, happen, with small brains and big breasts. She whips
him up the dancers once and that's the end of that. She likes the
colour of his uniform and that makes him feel big. Six months

before he was sitting behind a desk, copping on a weekly, picking his nose, and chatting up the pigeons on the window-sill. Now – all at once – he feels like he's a man. Before he knows where he is he's standing on the boat deck and the bint's waving him off from the docks with a bitsy hanky and tears clogging up her powder. My hero stuff. The captain blows the whistle on the bridge. The gang-plank's up. There's a military band on the quay-side, best boots and battledress, playing 'Where was the Engine Driver?' 'Goodbye Dolly I must leave you'. So there stands Charlie Harry, five foot four in his socks, and feeling like he's Clive of India, Alexander the Great, and Henry Five rolled into one.

MACLEISH: You're a real one for handing out the patter.

MITCHEM: Few weeks after that he's on his back with his feet in the air and a hole as big as your fist in his belly. And he's nothing.

MACLEISH [uneasily]: I reckon that it's you who thinks too much.

MITCHEM: I'm not a thinking kind of man. I look at facts. It happens to us all. Do you think that bint is going to float off to a nunnery? [Indicating the Prisoner] Just take a look at him. For all you know, his missis back in Tokyo thinks he's a sort of Rudolph Valentino.

MACLEISH: If she does she wants glasses.

MITCHEM: Happen so. But that's the way it is. So just you drop the home and bint and family bull. You might end up like him.

MACLEISH: How's that?

MITCHEM: What do you mean?

MACLEISH: So how does he end up when we head back?

MITCHEM: We're stacking him.

MACLEISH: That's what I understood. You mean we're leaving him behind.

MITCHEM: It's a sticky number as it is. We've got to go right through the lot of them. We'd never make it with a prisoner as well. It's odds against us now. With him as well we wouldn't stand a chance.

MACLEISH: I was beginning to get quite fond of him.

MITCHEM: He's no use now. He couldn't tell us any more than we know already. He's no cop to us. He's lost his value.

MACLEISH: Are we going to leave him here?

MITCHEM: Yeh.

MACLEISH: In the hut?

MITCHEM: That's right.

MACLEISH: That's a bit risky, isn't it?

MITCHEM: How do you mean?

MACLEISH: Suppose they find the track up here? Suppose the Japs come up and cut him loose? He lets them know what time we left. How many there are of us.

MITCHEM: He won't.

MACLEISH: Aye, but if he did? If they knew how much start we had on them they'd catch us up in no time. If he could tell them that . . .

MITCHEM: He won't.

MACLEISH: There's nothing to stop him.

MITCHEM: I've told you twice, he won't!

MACLEISH: I mean, it seems to me the risk's as big as if we tried to take him back with us. They know we're somewhere in this area. It's only a matter of time before they find this place.

MITCHEM: They don't know anything.

MACLEISH: They know we're round about here somewhere. Why else would they be bashing out the patter on the set?

MITCHEM: It's regular procedure with the Nips. Routine stuff. They push out muck in English on the off-chance. To put the wind up anyone who might be hanging round. It doesn't mean a thing.

MACLEISH: We won't have time to cover up the entrance of the track again. We'll have to go straight through. I mean, the path up here is going to be wide open. It's going to be like putting up a sign. The minute we move out of here it's ten to one they'll find the track straight off.

MITCHEM: They'll find him, that's all.

MACLEISH: Aye. But he can tell them. About us.

MITCHEM: He won't tell anybody. Anything.

MACLEISH: What's to stop him?

MITCHEM: I'll see to that.

MACLEISH: I fail to see what you can do about it.

MITCHEM: You don't have to.

MACLEISH: You're not . . . you're not going to knock him off?

MITCHEM: Just you do your job, Mac, that's all.

MACLEISH: You're not going to knock him off!

MITCHEM: Do you want to do it?

MACLEISH: He's a P.O.W.!

MITCHEM: Shut up.

MACLEISH: You can't kill him!

MITCHEM: That's my worry.

MACLEISH: The man's a prisoner-of-war!

MITCHEM: There's thousands more like him between this mob and base. It's him that's playing at home today, not you and me. If anybody's P.O.W.s it's us – not him.

MACLEISH: He gave himself up.

MITCHEM: He should have had more sense.

MACLEISH: You can't just walk him outside and put a bullet into him.

MITCHEM: No. I know that. It'd make too much noise.

MACLEISH [glancing down at the bayonet he holds in his hand]: Oh, God . . . Not that.

MITCHEM: Do you think I'm looking forward to it?

MACLEISH: Not that . . . Not like that.

MITCHEM: I've got six men and one report to come out of this lot. If I hang on to him it could work out I lose the whole patrol. I could lose more than that. For all we know, the unit's sitting back on its backside with thousands of these little Harries streaming down in that direction. You reckon I should lose my sleep over him?

MACLEISH: There must be something else.

MITCHEM: There isn't.

MACLEISH: There's another way.

MITCHEM: It's no good.

MACLEISH: Suppose we tied him up and ditched him in the bushes. Round the back, say. Out of sight. So it took a while for them to find him.

MITCHEM: It's no good!

MACLEISH: It's a damn sight better than doing him in.

MITCHEM: Is that what you think? Use your head. Do you think I haven't thought of that already? We hide him up out here he starves to death. That could take days. Do you think that's doing him a favour?

MACLEISH: What do you think you're doing?

MITCHEM: Me? My job. What they pay me to do.

MACLEISH: To knock off P.O.W.s!

MITCHEM: To put first things first.

MACLEISH: It's bloody murder, man!

MITCHEM [crossing to Macleish]: 'Course it is. That is my job. That's why I'm here. And you. [He indicates his stripes.] That's why I'm wearing these. And I'm wearing these 'cause I'm the one that makes decisions. Like this. If you want to do that, Jock, you can have my job right now. Here and now. It stinks. To me, it stinks. It stinks to me to do for him. But, come to that, the whole lot stinks to me. So what am I supposed to do? Turn conshi? Jack it in? Leave the world to his lot?

MACLEISH: I've got a brother who could just be sitting back – right now. Like him.

MITCHEM: Jock, I can smell your kind a mile away.

MACLEISH: What's that supposed to mean?

MITCHEM: The Bamforth touch.

MACLEISH: Bammo?

MITCHEM: You're as bad as Bamforth, boy.

MACLEISH: Me! You think that I'm like Bamforth?

MITCHEM: All the bloody way.

MACLEISH: You're off your nut.

MITCHEM: It's the book. According to the book. You can't forget the book. All along the road – the book. It doesn't work. You'd make a right pair. Nothing to choose between you – except that Bammo fiddles it to suit himself. You like to come the greater glory of mankind.

MACLEISH: It seems to me you're talking out of the back of your head.

MITCHEM: Don't you believe it. And to think that it was me who put you up for that tape. You're right – I must be going round the bend.

MACLEISH: You can strip me when you want. You know what you can do with the tape.

MITCHEM: And wouldn't that be lovely, eh? Wouldn't that just suit you down to the ground?

MACLEISH: How's that?

MITCHEM: It lets you out of this. On the ground floor. You're back in the ranks. One of the boys and none of the responsibility.

MACLEISH: Perhaps I'd rather be one of the boys.

MITCHEM: You can say that again. So why did you cop on for the tape in the first place?

MACLEISH: I've never complained about doing my job – that doesn't mean I'm willing to be a party to what you're suggesting.

MITCHEM: Lad, have you got lots to learn? How did you reckon it was going to be? Like in the comics? Fearless Mac Macleish charging up a little hill with a score of grenades and highland war cries? Wiping out machine guns single-handed? The gallant lance-jack gutting half a dozen Nips with a Boy Scout penknife and a Union Jack? Walking back to Jock-land with enough medals to sink a destroyer?

MACLEISH: You're talking through your hat.

MITCHEM [*crossing to Macleish*]: Yeh? Reckon, do you? Happen so. Perhaps you're right. You happen haven't got the guts for that. I'll tell you this much, boy – a touch like that's the easiest thing on earth. The army's full of square-head yobs who keep their brains between their legs. Blokes who do their nuts for fifteen seconds and cop a decoration, cheer boys cheer, Rule Britannia, and death before dishonour. All right. Why not? Good luck to them. Lads like that win wars so they should have the medals. They deserve them. But a touch like this comes harder. The trouble is with war – a lot of it's like this – most of it. Too much. You've that to learn.

MACLEISH: There's nothing you can teach me.

MITCHEM: You're dead right there.

MACLEISH: I make my own decisions.

MITCHEM: It's the only way. I'll just say this much, Jock: before you get much older you'll grow up. If this war shapes the way I think it will, you'll grow up, lad, in next to no time. [*He crosses towards table.*] Before the month is out you'll do a dozen jobs like this before you have your breakfast. [*He sits at table.*] So just think on.

WHITAKER [*turning at window*]: Sergeant Mitchem.

MITCHEM: You again? What is it now?

WHITAKER: I . . . I was wondering what the time was now.

MITCHEM: Not again! What's up? Do you want changing?

WHITAKER: It was just that I was wondering what time it was.

MITCHEM [*glances at his watch*]: Half past – all but.

WHITAKER: I thought it must be getting on that way.

MITCHEM: Another minute and I'll give the lads a shout.

[*The* PRISONER *gestures towards his breast pocket.*]

MACLEISH: Sarnt . . . Sergeant Mitchem!

MITCHEM [*glancing round*]: I ought to change my name. What's your complaint?

MACLEISH: It's him. I think there's something that he wants.

MITCHEM: If it's outside he can't. Tell him to hold it.

MACLEISH: Something in his pocket.

MITCHEM: Again? Oh – all right. O.K. See what it is. You get it for him.

MACLEISH: Right. [*To the Prisoner*] Now, you behave yourself, my lad. [MACLEISH *opens the Prisoner's breast pocket and extracts the wallet.*] Is this it? [*The* PRISONER *shakes his head.* MACLEISH *replaces the wallet and takes a cigarette case from the Prisoner's pocket.*] Is this it? Is it this that you were wanting? [*The* PRISONER *nods his head.*] Is it all right for the prisoner to have a drag, Sarge?

MITCHEM: Yeh. O.K.

MACLEISH [*he hands the case to the Prisoner who takes out two cigarettes, offering one to Macleish*]: Who? Me? You're giving one to me? [*He takes the proffered cigarette. The* PRISONER *closes the case and places it on the form.*] That's . . . that's very kind of you. [MACLEISH *takes a box of matches from his pocket.*] My name's Macleish. [*Points to himself*] Macleish. Do you understand? [*Pointing again to himself*] Macleish – me. [*He points to the Prisoner.*] Who – are – you? [*The* PRISONER *places his hands on his head.*] Is that the only thing you know?

MITCHEM [*crosses towards the sleeping figures of Bamforth, Evans, and*

Johnstone] : I shouldn't get too attached to him. [*He shakes Johnstone.*] Johnno! . . . Johnno!

[MACLEISH *gives the Prisoner a light behind the following dialogue.*]

JOHNSTONE [*wakes and sits up*] : Yeh?

MITCHEM: Half past.

JOHNSTONE [*rubs his eyes*] : Right.

MITCHEM [*crosses and shakes Bamforth*] : Come on, come on! Wakey-wakey, rise and shine. Let's have you! [BAMFORTH *sits up as* MITCHEM *crosses to wake Evans.*] Evans! Evans, lad!

EVANS [*sitting up*] : I feel horrible.

MITCHEM: You look it. Get your skates on. Let's be having you. The sun's burning your eyes out. Move yourselves, then!

EVANS: What's the time, Sarnt?

MITCHEM: Don't you start that as well. It's turned half past. [*He crosses to table and sits down, then glances across at Bamforth and Evans, who have not, as yet, made any attempt to rise.*] Come on! I said, move yourselves!

BAMFORTH: I've got a mouth like the inside of a tram driver's glove.

EVANS: Had a good kip, Bammo boy?

BAMFORTH: What? Kipping next to you? Kipping with a Taff? I'd rather bed down with an Eskimo's grannie. [*He lights a cigarette.*] I was having a smashing dream, though, son.

EVANS: Who was she?

BAMFORTH: Why should I tell you – you dream about your own. You dream about the milk-maids, Taff. They're more in your line. Have a sordid nightmare. The bints in my dreams have got class. Society bints.

EVANS: I bet they are.

BAMFORTH: Straight up.

JOHNSTONE: What do you know about society bints, Bamforth?

BAMFORTH: All the lot. You have to kiss them first.

[EVANS *laughs.*]

JOHNSTONE [*now on his feet*] : Got all the answers, haven't you?

BAMFORTH: Most of them. You've got to have with bints.

MITCHEM: All right, less of the love life, Bamforth. Let's have you on your feet.

[BAMFORTH *and* EVANS *rise and adjust their uniforms as* JOHN-STONE *crosses to the table.*]

JOHNSTONE: Anything fresh?

MITCHEM [*shakes his head*]: Not yet. We haven't tried the set again. Nothing new outside. [*He glances up as* BAMFORTH *crosses towards the door.*] What you on, then?

BAMFORTH [*at door*]: I want to go outside!

MITCHEM: What for?

BAMFORTH: I can't help it.

MITCHEM: I don't want anybody moving round outside.

BAMFORTH: It's not my fault!

MITCHEM: All right. Go on. And make it sharp.

BAMFORTH [*to Smith*]: So what am I supposed to do? Write out an application?

MITCHEM: If you're going, Bamforth, you'd better get off now.

BAMFORTH [*opens door*]: All right! [*To Smith*] So long.

EVANS [*crossing to stand by Smith*]: Bring me back a coconut, boy!

BAMFORTH [*as he exits*]: Fetch your own.

MITCHEM: Whitaker!

WHITAKER [*turning at window*]: Sarge?

MITCHEM: Cover him outside.

WHITAKER: Righto.

JOHNSTONE: What time we pushing off?

MITCHEM: Another half an hour, happen. Maybe more. As soon as it gets dark enough to give us cover.

JOHNSTONE [*inclining his head towards the Prisoner*]: And him?

MITCHEM: It's settled what we're going to do with him.

JOHNSTONE [*takes out a packet of cigarettes and offers one to Mitchem*]: Who?

MITCHEM [*shakes his head, declining the cigarette*]: Meaning what?

JOHNSTONE [*lights his own cigarette before answering*]: Who gets to do the job?

MITCHEM: Are you volunteering?

JOHNSTONE [*blows out a cloud of smoke*]: I don't mind.

MITCHEM: Do you know, I think you would at that.

JOHNSTONE: Somebody's got to do it.

MITCHEM: It's got to be arranged yet, has that. We could draw lots
I don't know – perhaps I ought to do the job myself.

JOHNSTONE: It wants doing quick.

MITCHEM: I know.

JOHNSTONE: And quiet.

MITCHEM: I know.

JOHNSTONE: It's a skilled job.

MITCHEM: I know all that!

JOHNSTONE: So it wants somebody who knows what they're doing
You or me. We could toss up.

MITCHEM: Look – don't try and teach me my job, eh?

JOHNSTONE: Only trying to help. Just making a suggestion. It wants
a professional touch. [*He glances across at the Prisoner who is still
smoking.*] Who gave him that?

MITCHEM: You what?

JOHNSTONE [*crosses and grasps the Prisoner's wrist*]: Macleish! Have
you been keeping him in smokes?

MITCHEM: I gave him permission.

JOHNSTONE [*releasing the Prisoner's hand in disgust*]: All right. Carry
on.

MACLEISH: I didn't give him the fag, in any case. [*He indicates his
own cigarette.*] As a matter of fact, it was him who gave me this.

JOHNSTONE: Going mates already?

MACLEISH: 'Course not.

JOHNSTONE: What's up then? Do you fancy him?

MACLEISH: I can't see that there's any harm in accepting a fag from
the bloke.

JOHNSTONE: You wouldn't.

MACLEISH: There's no harm in that!

JOHNSTONE: Not much. You ought to go the whole way, lad. Turn
native. You'll be eating your connor from banana leaves next. I
wouldn't touch his stinking wog tobacco.

MACLEISH: It's just an ordinary cigarette.

JOHNSTONE: You what? Let's have a shufti.

MACLEISH [*holding up his cigarette for Johnstone's inspection*]: It's just the
same as any other cigarette. There's no difference.

OHNSTONE [*taking the cigarette from Macleish*]: You wouldn't chuckle. It's the same all right. There's not a bit of difference. It's a Blighty fag. [*He snatches the cigarette from the Prisoner.*] They're British smokes. They're British army issue!

MITCHEM [*rising and crossing to join Johnstone*]: Give us hold. [JOHN-STONE *hands one of the cigarettes to Mitchem, who examines it closely.*] They're army issue right enough. He must have thieved them from the lads up country.

[MITCHEM, MACLEISH, *and* JOHNSTONE *turn and look at the Prisoner.*]

EVANS [*crossing to join the group*]: What's the matter, Jock? What's happened?

MACLEISH: It's him. It's bright boy there. He's carrying a load of British issue fags.

EVANS: How did he get hold of them?

JOHNSTONE: How do you think? You can have three guesses. The thieving Nip!

MITCHEM [*drops the cigarette and grinds it beneath his heel*]: If there's one thing gets my hump it's knocking off – it's looting.

JOHNSTONE [*holding out the cigarette to Macleish*]: Well, come on, Jock, you'd better finish it. You're the one he gave it to. You reckon you're his mate.

MACLEISH [*snatching the cigarette*]: I'll ram it down his rotten throat! I'll make him eat the rotten thing! [*He hesitates – for a moment we feel that he is about to carry out the threat – he hurls the cigarette across the room.*]

JOHNSTONE: You don't want to waste it, Jock. Not now you've started it. You never know how much that fag has cost. He's happen stuck his bayonet end in some poor Herb for that.

EVANS: There's some of them would kill their mothers for a drag.

MITCHEM [*to Macleish*]: And you were telling me how they treat P.O.W.S.

EVANS: He wants a lesson, Sarge. He ought to have a lesson taught to him.

MACLEISH: I'll kill him!

MITCHEM: Will you? You swop sides quick. [*There is a pause as they turn to look at the* PRISONER, *who, uncertain of their attitude towards him, picks up the case, opens it, and offers a cigarette to Mitchem.*] Stick 'em! [MITCHEM *strikes the case from the Prisoner's hand. The* PRISONER *raises his hands and places them on his head – on this occasion, however, the action is without humour.*] Thieving slob!

JOHNSTONE [*raising a fist*]: Who goes in first?

MITCHEM: Hold it.

JOHNSTONE [*advancing threateningly on the Prisoner*]: Who gets first crack?

MITCHEM: Hold it a sec.

[*Johnstone checks himself.*]

MACLEISH [*almost to himself*]: My brother's just nineteen. He's only been out here a couple of months. I haven't seen him since he docked. They whipped him straight up country. He's only just nineteen. [*A loud appeal to the patrol – as if in the hope of receiving a denial.*] For all I know he's dead!

MITCHEM: Jock – see 'f he's lugging anything else he's lifted from our lads.

MACLEISH [*moving to the Prisoner*]: Get up! Get on your feet! [*The* PRISONER *cowers on the form and* MACLEISH *jerks him savagely to his feet.*] Do as you're told! [MACLEISH *goes through the Prisoner's pocket and removes the wallet.*] There's this.

JOHNSTONE [*taking the wallet*]: I'll have a look at what's in this. You carry on.

MACLEISH [*as the Prisoner reacts slightly at the loss of the wallet*]: Stand still!

[MACLEISH *goes through the Prisoner's trouser pockets and removes the usual miscellaneous assortment of articles: handkerchief, keys, loose change, etc.* MACLEISH *places these on the form.* JOHNSTONE, *slowly and carefully, tears the photographs into pieces and drops these and the wallet on the floor. The* PRISONER *starts forward and* MACLEISH *rises and strikes him across the face.* BAMFORTH, *who has just re-entered from the veranda, notices this incident.*]

MACLEISH: I said, stand still!

BAMFORTH: What's up? What's he done to ask for that?

EVANS: He's been looting, Bammo. From our lads.

BAMFORTH [*crossing to join the group around the Prisoner*]: He's been what?

MACLEISH: We caught him with a fag-case stuffed with British army smokes!

BAMFORTH: You Scotch nit! You dim Scotch nit! I gave him them!

MITCHEM: You did?

BAMFORTH: I'm telling you. I gave him half a dozen snouts!

EVANS: You gave them him?

[MACLEISH *edges away from the Prisoner and* BAMFORTH *positions himself between the Prisoner and the members of the patrol.*]

BAMFORTH: What's the matter, Taff? Are your ears bad? I slipped him half a dozen nubs!

MACLEISH: I didn't know. I thought . . . I thought he'd knocked them off.

JOHNSTONE [*to Bamforth*]: And who gave you permission?

BAMFORTH: I've had this out with you before. You show where it says I have to grease up to an N.C.O. before I hand out fags. What's mine's my own. I decide what I do with it.

MACLEISH: How was I to know? I . . . I've told you, boy, I thought he'd knocked them off.

BAMFORTH: You know what thought did.

MACLEISH [*searching for words*]: How was I to know? . . . I mean, he gave one of them to me . . . I'd lit it up . . . I was having a drag . . . I was halfway down the lousy thing before I realized, you know – I mean, before I knew it was a Blighty fag . . . So how was I to feel? . . . What would you have done? . . . You tell me, Bammo . . . I could have choked, you know . . . I've got a brother who's up country.

BAMFORTH: If he's dropped in with a gang of Nips who think like you, God help the kiddie. God help him!

MACLEISH: I thought he'd looted them!

BAMFORTH: And so you pull the big brave hero bull. The raving highlander. Aren't you the boy? So what you waiting for? Well, come on, Jocko, finish off the job! [BAMFORTH *grabs the Prisoner, pinning his arms, and swings him round, holding him towards Macleish.*] Come on, come on! Come on, he's waiting for the hump. Let's see you slot him, Jock! Drop him one on! Let's see you do your stuff! Smash his face for him! Drop him one on!

MACLEISH: Lay off it, Bamforth.

MITCHEM: O.K., Bamforth, jack it in.

BAMFORTH: Haven't any of you got the guts to go the bundle? You were snapping at the leash when I walked in. What about you, Taff? You want to have a crack at him?

MITCHEM: I said drop it.

BAMFORTH [*loosing his hold on the Prisoner*]: I didn't start it.

[*The* PRISONER *sits on form and returns the articles to his trouser pockets.*]

EVANS: It was a mistake, Bammo.

BAMFORTH: You bet it was.

EVANS: We thought he'd whipped them.

BAMFORTH [*stoops and picks up the wallet and a piece of the torn photographs*]: You bastards. You even had to rip his pictures up. You couldn't leave him them even!

EVANS: I'll give you a hand to pick them up.

BAMFORTH: You couldn't even leave him them!

EVANS [*bends down and collects the torn pieces of the photographs*]: Happen he can stick them together again, Bammo. Here's a bit with a head on it. He could stick them together, easy enough, with a pot of paste and a brush.

BAMFORTH: Aw . . . Dry up, you Welsh burk.

EVANS [*rises and crosses to the Prisoner*]: Tojo . . . Tojo, boy. [*The* PRISONER *looks up.*] I got your pieces for you. You can stick them together again. Pot of paste and a bit of fiddling and they'll be right as rain. [MITCHEM *and* MACLEISH *move away from the Prisoner.*] Good as ever they was . . . Well, not quite as good happen, but if you don't mind the joins and do them careful it won't matter, will it? [EVANS *holds out the torn pieces, but the Prisoner, fearing further blows, is hesitant in accepting them.*] Go on, Tojo son, you have them back. Better than nothing, anyway. [*The* PRISONER *takes the torn fragments and examines them one by one.*] Some of them are only torn in two. All the face is there on that one. [*The* PRISONER *continues to examine the pieces.* EVANS *stoops to retrieve a scrap of a photograph which he had overlooked previously.*] A bit here I missed. Looks like a little bit of a little bit of a girlie. [*He examines the fragment closely.*] Oh no, it's a boy, is that. [*He presses the scrap into the hands of the Prisoner.*] You'll . . . you'll be needing that as well.

BAMFORTH [*handing the wallet to Evans*]: Here, Taff, stick him this.

EVANS: Right, boyo. [*He hands the wallet to the Prisoner.*] And here's your wallet, Tojo boy.

MACLEISH [*picks up the cigarette case from the floor and gives it to Bamforth*]: He's better have this back too. He'll . . . Maybe he'll be feeling in need of a smoke.

BAMFORTH: Yeh . . . Thanks, Jock. [*He crosses to return the cigarette case.*]

JOHNSTONE: Bamforth! Just a minute, lad.

BAMFORTH: Yeh?

JOHNSTONE: I'd like a look at that before you hand it on to him.

BAMFORTH: Ask him. Not me, It's his.

JOHNSTONE: He'll get it back. I only want it for a minute.

BAMFORTH [*hesitates, then crosses and hands the case to Johnstone*]: He'd better get it back.

JOHNSTONE: He will. [*He inspects the case, slowly turning it over in his hands, then tosses it to Bamforth.* BAMFORTH *crosses to return it to the Prisoner.*] Bamforth!

BAMFORTH [*turns*]: You want something else?

JOHNSTONE: No, lad. Nothing. I was just wondering, that's all.

BAMFORTH: Well?

JOHNSTONE: Are you feeling in a generous mood today?

BAMFORTH: What's that supposed to signify?

JOHNSTONE: Did you give him the case as well?

BAMFORTH: I gave him half a dozen fags, that's all. I haven't got a case myself to give away. I gave him half a dozen snouts, I've told you half a dozen times. The case belongs to him.

JOHNSTONE: Does it?

BAMFORTH: The case is his.

JOHNSTONE: That's interesting. You'd better have another shufti at it, then.

[BAMFORTH *inspects the case and is about to return it to the Prisoner.*]

MITCHEM: Pass it over, Bamforth.

BAMFORTH: What for? It's his.

MITCHEM: I'd like to once it over for myself.

BAMFORTH [*tosses the case to* MITCHEM, *who also examines it, then turns his glance upon the Prisoner*]: All right! So it's a British case!

JOHNSTONE: Made in Birmingham.

BAMFORTH: So what? What's that supposed to prove?

MITCHEM: So tell us now how he got hold of it.

BAMFORTH: I don't know. Don't ask me.

JOHNSTONE: I bloody do! The way he got the snouts.

BAMFORTH: I gave him the fags.

JOHNSTONE: So you say.

BAMFORTH: I gave him the fags!

MITCHEM: And what about the case?

BAMFORTH: Look – I don't know. I've told you – I don't know.

EVANS: So he has been on the lifting lark? Half-inching from the boys up country.

MACLEISH: It begins to look that way.

[MACLEISH *and* EVANS *move menacingly towards the Prisoner.*]

BAMFORTH [*planting himself between the Prisoner and Evans and Macleish*]: You've got it all sorted out between you.

EVANS: It stands to reason, man.

BAMFORTH: You ought to be in Scotland Yard, you lads. In Security.

MACLEISH: It's pretty obvious he's pinched the thing.

BAMFORTH: Is it?

EVANS: How else could he have got it, Bammo?

BAMFORTH: You pair of ignorant crones! Sherlock-Taffy-Bloody-Holmes and Charlie MacChan. Sexy Blake and his tartan boy assistant. How do I know where he got it from? It's you bright pair who seem to know the answers. You tell me. If I were you I'd have it cased for bloodstains and fingerprints with a magnifying glass. How does anybody cop on to a fag case? Eh? You buy them! In shops! With money! You know what money is, eh? Money, you know. The stuff they give you on a Friday night. Bits of paper and little round rings. That's the carry-on in my home town. Where you come from they still swop things for sheep.

MACLEISH: It's a British case, Bamforth.

BAMFORTH: You're a head case, Jock. I've got a little skin and blister back in Blighty. Twelve years old. She carts around a squinting Nippo doll. Know how she got it? One night, instead of being tucked up in her little bed, she was out roaming the streets with a chopper. She knocked off nine Nippo nippers in a night nursery and nicked a golliwog, two teddy-bears, and this here doll. You want to know how we found out? It's got 'Made in Japan' stamped across it's pink behind. Now, work that one out.

MITCHEM: It won't wash, Bamforth. The Nips don't import fancy swag. They churn it out themselves and flog it abroad.

BAMFORTH [*stepping aside to give Macleish and Evans access to the Prisoner*]: All right! Go on. Beat him up, then. Work him over. Enjoy yourselves for once. Have a good time. Look – listen. You want to know something? You want to know who's got the biggest hoard of loot in the Far East, bar none? Who's collected more Jap swag than any regiment? I'll introduce him. [BAMFORTH *crosses to rear of hut and raises Whitaker's hand.*] On my right and stepping in the ring at six stone six – the terror of the Newcastle Church Army Hostel: Private Winnie Whitaker!

WHITAKER [*embarrassed at being drawn into the proceedings*]: Cut it out, Bammo.

BAMFORTH: Take a bow, son. Here he is. The sole proprietor of the Samuel Whitaker War Museum. It's worth hard gelt in anybody's lingo.

[WHITAKER *manages to extricate his hand from Bamforth's grip.*]

MITCHEM: What are you getting at?

BAMFORTH: Ask the boy himself. He's the proud possessor. Come on, Whitaker, my old son, don't be bashful. Tell them all about your battle honours. What you did in the war, dad.

WHITAKER: I don't know what you're supposed to be talking about.

BAMFORTH: Don't you? Smudger knows. Smudger's seen it. He can bear me out.

SMITH: Leave the kid alone, Bammo. There's no harm in it.

BAMFORTH: It's true, isn't it?

SMITH: Look – lay off the lad.

BAMFORTH: Is it the truth?

SMITH: Yes . . . He's got a bit of swag.

BAMFORTH: A bit! That's the bloody understatement of the war, is that.

WHITAKER: It's only souvenirs, Bammo.

EVANS: What kind of souvenirs you got, Sammy?

BAMFORTH: He's got it in his locker back at camp. Smudge and me had a shufti one morning when he left it open. Well, come on Whitto, don't be shy. Tell them what you've got.

WHITAKER: Just some odds and ends, man, and a few things I've picked up, that's all.

BAMFORTH: Tell them!

WHITAKER: Some Jap buttons and a couple of rounds.

BAMFORTH: And the rest.

WHITAKER: A nippo cap badge and a belt.

BAMFORTH: Go on.

WHITAKER: That's all.

BAMFORTH: I've seen inside your locker.

WHITAKER: That's all there is.

BAMFORTH: You're lying, Whitaker!

WHITAKER: I'm not, man. I've not got anything else.

BAMFORTH: You're a lying get!

WHITAKER: Only some bits and pieces.

SMITH: Let him alone, Bamforth.

BAMFORTH: His locker's loaded with Jap loot. It's like a little Tokyo inside his locker.

WHITAKER: They're only souvenirs, Bammo.

BAMFORTH: Don't give me that. There's half the emperor's arsenal and the Imperial quartermaster's stores in there. When you get home with that lot, Whitaker, you won't half give the family the bull. Will you be able to chat them up, boy, on how you won the war. The Tyneside hero. [*To Evans and Macleish*] And you lot want to string the fives on Tojo just because he's got a Blighty fag case. If the Nips lay hands on Whitaker they'll work it out that he's a sort of military Al Capone. Him! Whitaker! Whining Whitaker! The boy who has a nervous breakdown at the thought of Madame

Butterfly. Show him a rice pudding and he gets the screaming ab-
dabs. He's never even seen a Jap excepting that one there.

SMITH: Can't you leave the lad alone?

BAMFORTH: All right. I've done with him. But just for the book,
Whitaker, just to put these boys here right – just tell them how you
copped on to the spoils of war.

WHITAKER: I don't know. I just . . . they just came into my posses-
sion.

BAMFORTH: Tell them how!

WHITAKER: I swopped some things for them. In the NAAFI. Down
the U.J. club. I swopped them for some stuff I had myself – with
some blokes I met who'd come down from up country.

BAMFORTH: That's all I want to know.

WHITAKER: It's not a crime.

BAMFORTH: No. No, it's not a crime. [*Crossing down-stage*] It's not a
crime to have a fag case either. Now, go on, Jock, beat up the Nip.

MACLEISH: You still haven't proved, to my satisfaction, that that's
the way he got the case.

BAMFORTH: You try and prove it different.

MACLEISH [*turning away from the Prisoner*]: . . . Och, what's it matter,
anyway . . .

MITCHEM: Evans!

EVANS: Sarge?

MITCHEM [*tossing the cigarette case to Evans*]: You'd better give him
this back.

EVANS: Righto.

[EVANS *gives the case to the* PRISONER, *who opens it, takes out a
cigarette, and offers one to* EVANS, *who hesitates and then accepts.*
EVANS *takes out a box of matches and gives the Prisoner a light.*]

WHITAKER [*desiring to change the conversation*]: Sergeant Mitchem . . .

MITCHEM: What's your worry?

WHITAKER: I was wondering about the time . . .

MITCHEM: Do you ever do anything else?

WHITAKER: I mean about reliefs. For Smudger and myself. It's well
turned half past now.

MITCHEM: I know! . . . All right. Who's next for stag?

75

MACLEISH [*collects his rifle and crosses to rear*]: Me, for one.

MITCHEM: Take over from Ticker Whitaker before he does his nut.

WHITAKER: I only mentioned it in case it might have slipped your memory, Sarge.

MITCHEM: Tick, tick, tick! You should have been a bloody clock.

WHITAKER [*having been relieved by Macleish, he crosses down-stage*]: I wasn't complaining. I thought you'd forgotten.

MITCHEM: I'm not likely to with you around. [*Points to his watch*] If ever this packs in on me I'll wrap you around my wrist. Evans!

EVANS: Sarge?

MITCHEM: Give Smudge a break. [*Indicating the Prisoner*] Bamforth, you just keep an eye on him.

BAMFORTH: He's all right.

MITCHEM: Just keep an eye on him, that's all.

EVANS [*collects his rifle and crosses towards Smith. As he approaches he shoulders his rifle and carries out a 'cod' guard mounting routine with exaggerated smartness. SMITH obeys the orders*]: Old guard . . . 'shun! Stand at . . . ease! 'Shun! . . . Slope . . . Arms! One – two-three, one – two-three, one! . . . Order . . . arms! One – two-three, one – two-three, one! Very good, Smudger boy. You should have joined the Guards. The sentries will now dismiss for a crafty smoke and a bit of abuse in the boiler house . . . old guard – to the guard room . . . Dis . . .

JOHNSTONE: All right, Evans. Cut out the funny stuff.

EVANS: You see how it is, Smudger? When you try to be regimental they won't have it. O.K., boyo, you scarper. I'll take over here.

SMITH: It's all yours, Taff.

[EVANS *takes up his position at the window as* SMITH *crosses down-stage.* WHITAKER *and* SMITH *prop their rifles against the wall.*]

WHITAKER: Hey, Taff!

EVANS: What is it, boy?

WHITAKER: Can I have a look at your book? That one you were reading out of earlier on?

EVANS: In my small pack, Whitto.

WHITAKER [*crossing to take magazine from Evans's pack which is on the form by the Prisoner*]: Thanks, Taffy.

BAMFORTH [*as* WHITAKER *gives the Prisoner a wide berth*] : It's all right, Whitto, he won't bite you, son. [BAMFORTH *watches* WHITAKER *as he takes the magazine from the pack and settles himself on the extreme end of the form.*] You trying to improve your mind?

WHITAKER: I just wanted to pass a few minutes on. [*He flicks through the pages.*] Where's that story that Taff was telling us about? The one with the Arabs.

SMITH: It's a serial, Sammy. No good starting that.

WHITAKER: I don't mind. It's something to read.

BAMFORTH: You screw the pictures, Whitaker. No good stuffing your head up with them long words. Have a butcher's at the corset adverts on the last page.

SMITH: He's not old enough for them.

BAMFORTH: He's got to start sometime. He can't stay ignorant for ever.

WHITAKER: Who's ignorant?

BAMFORTH: You are! Ignorant as a pig. Pig-ignorant, boy, that's you.

WHITAKER: That's all you know, Bamforth.

BAMFORTH: Hark at him! The innocent abroad. The voice of experience. They lock their daughters up in Newcastle when he's on leave. Go on, Whitaker, you've never been with a bint in your life.

WHITAKER: That just shows how much you know, boy!

SMITH: Never mind him, Sammy. He's pulling your leg.

WHITAKER: He doesn't know so much himself.

BAMFORTH: Have you ever had a woman, Whitaker?

WHITAKER: 'Course I have. I was courting when I left Blighty.

BAMFORTH: I bet.

SMITH: Newcastle girl, Sammy?

WHITAKER: No. Darlington lass. I met her at a dance once when I was stationed at Catterick.

BAMFORTH: Dancing! Get him! He'll be drinking beer and playing cards for money next.

WHITAKER: It was in a church hall – the dance, I mean. One of the lads in the billet took me. That's how I met this girl.

SMITH: Got a photograph?

WHITAKER: I've got a couple back at camp.

SMITH: What's she like? Bramah, eh?

WHITAKER: She's ... well, she's sort of pretty, you know, like. Mary. That's her name. Mary Pearson. Comes up to about my shoulder and sort of yellowish hair. Works for an insurance company. In the office. Oh, she's ... she's bloody pretty, Smudge. Nothing outstanding, like – but, boy, she's pretty. We was courting for three months very nearly. I was up there doing my basic training.

SMITH: Take her out much, did you?

WHITAKER: I used to get to meet her a couple of times a week, like. Whenever I could skive off. Get the bus from the camp centre into Darlington and meet her nights outside a shop. Some nights we'd go to the pictures – or dancing – or something – when I could afford it, like. I wasn't loaded them days. So most nights we'd just walk up through the park, you know. Along by the river. The middle of summer I was at Catterick. Was it hot then, boy! Oh, man ...! She's only seventeen just – is it a bit young, do you think?

SMITH: Doesn't seem to make much difference – these days.

WHITAKER: So we'd just walk along by the side of the river, like. Up as far as the bridge. Happen sit down and watch them playing bowls. Sit for ten minutes or so, get up and walk back. Just a steady stroll, you know. I never had much money – only my bus fare there and back sometimes – but it was ... Oh, boy! Oh, you know – we had some smashing times together, me and her. I wish I was back there now, boy.

SMITH: Write to her, do you?

WHITAKER: When I get the chance. When I'm back in camp. Every day if I've got the time.

SMITH: Roll on the duration, eh?

WHITAKER: I used to hear from her twice a week. I haven't had a letter for over a month. Almost six weeks.

SMITH: You know how it is, Sammy. Maybe she's busy.

WHITAKER: I don't know. I'm thinking happen she's got fixed up with another bloke.

SMITH: Maybe the mail's been held up.

WHITAKER: I get plenty from my mother and the old man. I think it's another bloke she's with.

SMITH: You don't want to think like that.

WHITAKER: The letters – the writing – things she said – it was different. Towards the last one, like.

SMITH: Happen be one waiting for you when you get back tomorrow.

WHITAKER: Aye. Happen so . . . I don't know. I've sort of given up, like. Hoping, you know.

[*It is early evening and the light has begun to dim. The jungle is silent and a stillness falls upon the patrol.* BAMFORTH *begins to sing – quietly and with a touch of sadness.*]

BAMFORTH: A handsome young private lay dying,
　　　At the edge of the jungle he lay.
　　　The Regiment gathered round him,
　　　To hear for the last words he'd say.
　　　'Take the trigger-guard out of my kidneys,
　　　Take the magazine out of my brain,
　　　Take the barrel from out of my back-bone,
　　　And assemble my rifle again . . .'

[*In an attempt to restore the previous mood,* BAMFORTH *rubs the top of the Prisoner's head playfully.*] Now then, Tojo, my old flowerpot, what did you think of that? That's better than you cop on from the Tokyo geisha fillies.

EVANS [*turning at window*]: It'll not be long before it's dark now, Sarge.

MACLEISH [*without turning from window*]: It's quiet out there. It's bloody quiet.

MITCHEM [*rising*]: Time we got ready for the push then. Got packed up. Got things – sorted out.

BAMFORTH [*having taken a swig from his water bottle, he wipes the lip and offers the bottle to the Prisoner*]: Come on, Tojo son. Get a gob of this before we go.

[*The* PRISONER *accepts the bottle gratefully.*]

JOHNSTONE: There's no more buckshees for the Nippo, Bamforth.

[*The* PRISONER, *sensing the meaning from Johnstone's tone, returns the water bottle to Bamforth without drinking.*]

BAMFORTH [*puts down the water bottle and turns to face Johnstone*]: I've warned you, Johnno. Don't overstep them tapes. I'll not take any more of the patter. Is it O.K. if I give the prisoner a drink, Sarge?

MITCHEM: You heard what Corporal Johnstone said, Bamforth.

BAMFORTH [*incredulous*]: You what?

JOHNSTONE: There's no more water for the Nippo.

BAMFORTH: Like hell there isn't. The bloke's got to drink.

MITCHEM: He's had a drink – earlier on this afternoon. I gave him one myself.

BAMFORTH: He's not a camel!

MITCHEM: I'm sorry, Bamforth. We've none to spare for him.

BAMFORTH: Sorry!

MITCHEM: We'll need every drop we've got for getting back. It's dead certain there'll be a gang of Nips around every water hole from here to base.

BAMFORTH: So we share out what we've got.

MITCHEM: No.

BAMFORTH: He gets half of mine.

MITCHEM: No! There's none for him.

BAMFORTH: He'll have to have a drink sometime. He can't go the distance without – you've got to get him back as well. [*He waits for a reply.*] We're taking him as well!

MITCHEM: I'm sorry.

JOHNSTONE: He's stopping where he is. [*He picks up the Prisoner's bayonet from the table.*] It's cobblers for him.

BAMFORTH: No.

MITCHEM: I've got no choice.

BAMFORTH: You said he was going back.

MITCHEM: He was – before. The circumstances altered. The situation's changed. I can't take him along.

BAMFORTH: What's the poor get done to us?

MITCHEM: It's a war. It's something in a uniform and it's a different shade to mine.

BAMFORTH [*positioning himself between the Prisoner and Johnstone*]: You're not doing it, Johnno.

JOHNSTONE: You laying odds on that?

BAMFORTH: For Christ's sake!

JOHNSTONE: It's a bloody Nip.

BAMFORTH: He's a man!

JOHNSTONE [*crossing a few paces towards the Prisoner*]: Shift yourself, Bamforth. Get out of the way.

BAMFORTH: You're not doing it.

MITCHEM: Bamforth, shift yourself.

BAMFORTH: You're a bastard, Mitchem.

MITCHEM: I wish to God I was.

BAMFORTH: You're a dirty bastard, Mitchem.

MITCHEM: As far as I'm concerned, it's all these lads or him.

BAMFORTH: It's him and me.

MITCHEM [*crossing to join Johnstone*]: Get to one side. That's an order.

BAMFORTH: Stick it.

MITCHEM: For the last time, Bamforth, move over.

BAMFORTH: Try moving me.

MITCHEM: I've not got time to mess about.

BAMFORTH: So come on, Whitaker! Don't sit there, lad. Who's side you on? [WHITAKER *rises slowly from the form. For a moment it would seem that he is going to stand by Bamforth but he crosses the room to stand beyond Mitchem and Johnstone.*] You've got no guts, Whitaker. You know that, boy? You've just got no guts.

WHITAKER: We've got to get back, Bammo.

BAMFORTH: You're a gutless slob!

WHITAKER: I've got to get back!

BAMFORTH: Evans. Taffy, Taff! [EVANS *turns from the window.*] Put the gun on these two, son.

EVANS: I reckon Mitch is right, you know. We couldn't get him back to camp, could we, boyo? The Nips must have a Div between the camp and us.

BAMFORTH: He's going to kill him, you nit!

EVANS: You never know about that fag case, do you, son?

BAMFORTH: What's the fag case got to do with it! ... Smudger! Smudger, now it's up to you.

SMITH: Don't ask me, Bammo. Leave me out of it.

BAMFORTH: You're in it, Smudge. You're in it up to here.

SMITH: I just take orders. I just do as I'm told. I just plod on.

BAMFORTH: The plodding on has stopped. Right here. Right here you stop and make a stand. He's got a wife and kids.

SMITH: I've got a wife and kids myself. Drop it, Bammo, it's like Mitch says – it's him or us.

BAMFORTH: Jock! . . . Jock! [MACLEISH *continues to stare out of the window.*] Macleish! . . . [MACLEISH *does not move.*] I hope they carve your brother up. Get that? I hope they carve your bloody brother up!

MITCHEM: All right, Bamforth, you've had your say. Now shift.

BAMFORTH: Shift me! Come on, heroes, shift me!

MITCHEM: Whitaker! Grab a gun and cover the Nip.

BAMFORTH: Don't do it, Whitaker. Stay out of it.

MITCHEM: Whitaker!

[WHITAKER *picks up a sten from the table and crosses to cover the Prisoner, who has realized the implications and is trembling with fear.* MITCHEM *and* JOHNSTONE *move forward to overpower Bamforth.* JOHNSTONE *drops the bayonet on the floor and, together with* MITCHEM, *grapples with* BAMFORTH. *As they fight the* PRISONER *begins to rise to his feet.*]

WHITAKER [*already in a state of fear himself*]: Get down! . . . Sit down! . . . [*The* PRISONER *continues to rise.*] Sit down, you stupid man, or I'll have to put a bullet into you . . . [*The* PRISONER *is standing upright as* WHITAKER'S *finger tightens on the trigger. A long burst from the sten shudders the hut and the bullets slam home into the body of the Prisoner like hammer blows. The* PRISONER *doubles up and falls to the floor. The fight stops. There is a pause.* WHITAKER *drops the sten and buries his face in his hands.*] God . . . God . . . God . . . [*His voice swells.*] Oh, God!

MITCHEM: Well, that should roust out every Nip from here to Tokyo. You've made a mess of that, lad. [WHITAKER, *uncompre-hending, looks at his hands.* MITCHEM *seizes him by the shoulders and shakes him savagely.*] Come on, come on! Come out of it! He's just the first.

BAMFORTH: You've got the biggest souvenir of all. You've done it this time, Whitaker. Take that and hang it on the front room wall . . .

[*Bamforth's words are cut short as* MITCHEM *strikes him across the face.*]

MITCHEM: We've had enough from you.

[EVANS *and* MACLEISH *have left their posts and, together with* SMITH, *are drawn in fascination towards the body of the Prisoner.*]

JOHNSTONE: All right. Get back. It's just a corpse. You'll see a whole lot more like that before you've done.

MITCHEM: Right. All of you. We're moving out. In double time. Get your gear together. Thirty seconds and we're off. Any longer and this place will be rotten with Nips. Any man not ready stays behind. Move!

[*The members of the patrol put on their packs, ammunition pouches, etc.*]

MITCHEM: Johnno, ditch your stuff. Can you work the set? [JOHNSTONE *nods assent and crosses to radio.*] Give it one last crack. [JOHNSTONE *switches on the set and the crackle of interference grows behind.*] We haven't got a snowball's chance in Hell of getting back. So try and let them know the Japs have broken through.

JOHNSTONE [*nods and switches to 'transmit'*]: Blue Patrol calling Red Leader . . . Blue Patrol calling Red Leader . . . Are you receiving me . . . Are you receiving me . . . Come in Red Leader . . . Over . . . [JOHNSTONE *switches to 'receive' and the interference swells.*] . . . Not a rotten peep.

MITCHEM: All right. Jack it in.

JOHNSTONE [*rips off headphones, leaving the set switched on. He straps on his ammunition pouches and picks up the sten from the floor.*]: Let's have you then! We're pushing off!

MITCHEM [*picking up his own sten*]: Leave what you haven't got. And move!

[*The members of the patrol collect their rifles and cross to the door.* JOHNSTONE *glances out of the window.*]

JOHNSTONE: All clear.

MITCHEM [*opens the door*]: I'll break the trail, Johnno, you bring up the rear. [JOHNSTONE *nods.*] All right, let's go.

[*One by one the members of the patrol follow* MITCHEM *through the door.* JOHNSTONE *is the last to leave. As the door closes behind Johnstone the interference increases on the set and suddenly it bursts into life.*]

OPERATOR [*on distort*]: . . . Red Leader calling Blue Patrol . . . Red Leader calling Blue Patrol . . . Come in Blue Patrol . . . Come in Blue Patrol . . . Over . . .

[*A machine gun chatters in the jungle and is joined by another. We hear the sound of one or two rifles and the screams of dying men. The noise of gunfire fades away, to leave only the whimper of one wounded man— it is Whitaker. The door is pushed open and* JOHNSTONE *enters. He has a bullet wound in his side and the blood is seeping through his shirt. Slamming the door shut, he leans upon it to regain his breath.*]

WHITAKER [*screams out from the jungle in fear*]: God! . . . God! . . .

[*A final cry of terror louder than any we have heard previously.*] Mother . . .!

[*We hear the sound of a single shot and Whitaker is dead.* JOHN-STONE *presses his hand to his side. The set splutters into life again.*]

OPERATOR [*on distort*]: . . . Are you receiving me, Blue Patrol . . . Are you receiving me . . . Over . . .

JOHNSTONE [*crosses slowly to the set, picks up hand-set, and switches to 'transmit'*]: Get knotted! All of you! You hear! The whole damn lot of you!

[JOHNSTONE *switches off the set and crosses towards the body of the Prisoner. As he passes the window there is a short burst of machine-gun fire. He ducks below window level. Squatting by the side of the body, he takes the cigarette case from the Prisoner's pocket and helps himself to a cigarette. Sticking the cigarette in his mouth, he returns the case to the Prisoner's pocket. He tugs the white silk scarf, now spattered with blood, from the Prisoner's neck and crawls across to beneath the window, where he ties the scarf round the barrel of his sten. It has all required a great effort, and he lights the cigarette and inhales deeply before continuing. Squatting below the window, he waves the white flag and, in turn, takes long pulls at the cigarette. For a moment there is complete silence and then a bird sings out in the jungle.*]

CURTAIN

HAROLD PINTER

The Dumb Waiter

THE DUMB WAITER

First presented at the Hampstead Theatre Club on 21 January 1960, with the following cast:

BEN   Nicholas Selby
GUS   George Tovey

THE DUMB WAITER was subsequently presented at the Royal Court Theatre on 8 March 1960 with the same cast.

Scene: A basement room. Two beds, flat against the back wall. A serving hatch, closed, between the beds. A door to the kitchen and lavatory, left. A door to a passage, right.

[*BEN is lying on a bed, reading a paper. GUS is sitting on a bed, right, tying his shoelaces, with difficulty. Both are dressed in shirts, trousers, and braces. Silence.*

GUS ties his laces, rises, yawns, and begins to walk slowly to the door, left. He stops, looks down, and shakes his foot. BEN lowers his paper and watches him. GUS kneels and unties his shoe-lace and slowly takes off the shoe. He looks inside it and brings out a flattened matchbox. He shakes it and examines it. Their eyes meet. BEN rattles his paper and reads. GUS puts the matchbox in his pocket and bends down to put on his shoe. He ties his lace, with difficulty. BEN lowers his paper and watches him. GUS walks to the door, left, stops, and shakes the other foot. He kneels, unties his shoe-lace, and slowly takes off the shoe. He looks inside it and brings out a flattened cigarette packet. He shakes it and examines it. Their eyes meet. BEN rattles his paper and reads. GUS puts the packet in his pocket, bends down, puts on his shoe, and ties the lace. He wanders off, left.

BEN slams the paper down on the bed and glares after him. He picks up the paper and lies on his back, reading.

Silence.

A lavatory chain is pulled twice, off left, but the lavatory does not flush. Silence.

GUS re-enters, left, and halts at the door, scratching his head. BEN slams down the paper.]

BEN: Kaw! [*He picks up the paper.*] What about this? [*He refers to the paper.*] A man of eighty-seven wanted to cross the road. But there was a lot of traffic, see? He couldn't see how he was going to squeeze through. So he crawled under a lorry.

GUS: He what?

BEN: He crawled under a lorry. A stationary lorry.

GUS: No?

BEN: The lorry started and ran over him.

GUS: Go on!

BEN: That's what it says here.

GUS: Get away.

BEN: It's enough to make you want to puke, isn't it?

GUS: Who advised him to do a thing like that?

BEN: A man of eighty-seven crawling under a lorry!

GUS: It's unbelievable.

BEN: It's down here in black and white.

GUS: Incredible.

[*Silence.* GUS *shakes his head and exits.* BEN *lies back and reads. The lavatory chain is pulled once off left, but the lavatory does not flush.* BEN *whistles at an item in the paper.* GUS *re-enters.*]

I want to ask you something.

BEN: What are you doing out there?

GUS: Well, I was just –

BEN: What about the tea?

GUS: I'm just going to make it.

BEN: Well, go on, make it.

GUS: Yes, I will. [*He sits in a chair. Ruminatively*] He's laid on some very nice crockery this time, I'll say that. It's sort of striped. There's a white stripe.

[BEN *reads.*]

It's very nice. I'll say that.

[BEN *turns the pages.*]

You know, sort of round the cup. Round the rim. All the rest of it's black, you see. Then the saucer's black, except for right in the middle, where the cup goes, where it's white.

[BEN *reads.*]

Then the plates are the same, you see. Only they've got a black stripe – the plates – right across the middle. Yes, I'm quite taken with the crockery.

BEN [*still reading*]: What do you want plates for? You're not going to eat.

GUS: I've brought a few biscuits.

BEN: Well, you'd better eat them quick.

GUS: I always bring a few biscuits. Or a pie. You know I can't drink tea without anything to eat.

BEN: Well, make the tea, then, will you? Time's getting on.

[GUS *brings out the flattened cigarette packet and examines it.*]

GUS: You got any cigarettes? I think I've run out. [*He throws the packet high up and leans forward to catch it.*] I hope it won't be a long job, this one. [*Aiming carefully, he flips the packet under his bed.*] Oh, I wanted to ask you something.

BEN [*slamming his paper down*]: Kaw!

GUS: What's that?

BEN: A child of eight killed a cat!

GUS: Get away.

BEN: It's a fact. What about that, eh? A child of eight killing a cat!

GUS: How did he do it?

BEN: It was a girl.

GUS: How did she do it?

BEN: She – [*He picks up the paper and studies it.*] It doesn't say.

GUS: Why not?

BEN: Wait a minute. It just says – Her brother, aged eleven, viewed the incident from the toolshed.

GUS: Go on!

BEN: That's bloody ridiculous.

[*Pause.*]

GUS: I bet he did it.

BEN: Who?

GUS: The brother.

BEN: I think you're right. [*Pause. Slamming down the paper*] What about that, eh? A kid of eleven killing a cat and blaming it on his little sister of eight! It's enough to – [*He breaks off in disgust and seizes the paper.* GUS *rises.*]

GUS: What time is he getting in touch?

[BEN *reads.*]

What time is he getting in touch?

BEN: What's the matter with you? It could be any time. Any time.

GUS [*moves to the foot of Ben's bed*]: Well, I was going to ask you something.

BEN: What?

GUS: Have you noticed the time that tank takes to fill?

BEN: What tank?

GUS: In the lavatory.

BEN: No. Does it?

GUS: Terrible.

BEN: Well, what about it?

GUS: What do you think's the matter with it?

BEN: Nothing.

GUS: Nothing?

BEN: It's got a deficient ballcock, that's all.

GUS: A deficient what?

BEN: Ballcock.

GUS: No? Really?

BEN: That's what I should say.

GUS: Go on! That didn't occur to me. [GUS *wanders to his bed and presses the mattress.*] I didn't have a very restful sleep today, did you? It's not much of a bed. I could have done with another blanket too. [*He catches sight of a picture on the wall.*] Hello, what's this? [*Peering at it.*] 'The First Eleven.' Cricketers. You seen this, Ben?

BEN [*reading*]: What?

GUS: The first eleven.

BEN: What?

GUS: There's a photo here of the first eleven.

BEN: What first eleven?

GUS [*studying the photo*]: It doesn't say.

BEN: What about that tea?

GUS: They all look a bit old to me. [GUS *wanders downstage, looks out front, then all about the room.*] I wouldn't like to live in this dump. I wouldn't mind if you had a window, you could see what it looked like outside.

BEN: What do you want a window for?

GUS: Well, I like to have a bit of a view, Ben. It whiles away the time. [*He walks about the room.*] I mean, you come into a place when it's still dark, you come into a room you've never seen before, you sleep all day, you do your job, and then you go away in the night again. [*Pause.*] I like to get a look at the scenery. You never get the chance in this job.

BEN: You get your holidays, don't you?

GUS: Only a fortnight.

BEN [*lowering the paper*]: You kill me. Anyone would think you're working every day. How often do we do a job? Once a week? What are you complaining about?

GUS: Yes, but we've got to be on tap though, haven't we? You can't move out of the house in case a call comes.

BEN: You know what your trouble is?

GUS: What?

BEN: You haven't got any interests.

GUS: I've got interests.

BEN: What? Tell me one of your interests.

[*Pause.*]

GUS: I've got interests.

BEN: Look at me. What have I got?

GUS: I don't know. What?

BEN: I've got my woodwork. I've got my model boats. Have you ever seen me idle? I'm never idle. I know how to occupy my time, to its best advantage. Then when a call comes, I'm ready.

GUS: Don't you ever get a bit fed-up?

BEN: Fed up? What with?

[*Silence.*]

[BEN *reads.* GUS *feels in the pocket of his jacket, which hangs on the bed.*]

GUS: You got any cigarettes? I've run out.

[*The lavatory flushes off left.*]

There she goes. [GUS *sits on his bed.*] No, I mean, I say the crockery's good. It is. It's very nice. But that's about all I can say for this place. It's worse than the last one. Remember that last place we were in? Last time, where was it? At least there was a wireless there. No, honest. He doesn't seem to bother much about our comfort these days.

BEN: When are you going to stop jabbering?

GUS: You'd get rheumatism in a place like this, if you stayed long.

BEN: We're not staying long. Make the tea, will you? We'll be on the job in a minute.

[GUS *picks up a small bag by his bed and brings out a packet of tea. He examines it and looks up.*]

GUS: Eh, I've been meaning to ask you.

BEN: What the hell is it now?

GUS: Why did you stop the car this morning, in the middle of that road?

BEN [*lowering the paper*]: I thought you were asleep.

GUS: I was, but I woke up when you stopped. You did stop, didn't you? [*Pause.*] In the middle of that road. It was still dark, don't you remember? I looked out. It was all misty. I thought perhaps you wanted to kip, but you were sitting up dead straight, like you were waiting for something.

BEN: I wasn't waiting for anything.

GUS: I must have fallen asleep again. What was all that about then? Why did you stop?

BEN [*picking up the paper*]: We were too early.

GUS: Early? [*He rises.*] What do you mean? We got the call, didn't we, saying we were to start right away. We did. We shoved out on the dot. So how could we be too early?

BEN [*quietly*]: Who took the call, me or you?

GUS: You.

BEN: We were too early.

GUS: Too early for what? [*Pause.*] You mean someone had to get out before we got in? [*He examines the bedclothes.*] I thought these sheets didn't look too bright. I thought they ponged a bit. I was too tired to notice when I got in this morning. Eh, that's taking a bit of a liberty, isn't it? I didn't want to share my bed-sheets. I told you things were going down the drain. I mean, we've always had clean sheets laid on up till now. I've noticed it.

BEN: How do you know those sheets weren't clean?

GUS: What do you mean?

BEN: How do you know they weren't clean? You've spent the whole day in them, haven't you?

GUS: What, you mean it might be my pong? [*He sniffs sheets.*] Yes. [*He sits slowly on bed.*] It could be my pong, I suppose. It's difficult to tell. I don't really know what I pong like, that's the trouble.

BEN [*referring to the paper*]: Kaw!

GUS: Eh, Ben.

BEN: Kaw!

GUS: Ben.

BEN: What?

GUS: What town are we in? I've forgotten.

BEN: I've told you. Birmingham.

GUS: Go on! [*He looks with interest about the room.*] That's in the Midlands. The second biggest city in Great Britain. I'd never have guessed. [*He snaps his fingers.*] Eh, it's Friday today, isn't it? It'll be Saturday tomorrow.

BEN: What about it?

GUS [*excited*]: We could go and watch the Villa.

BEN: They're playing away.

GUS: No, are they? Caarr! What a pity.

BEN: Anyway, there's no time. We've got to get straight back.

GUS: Well, we have done in the past, haven't we? Stayed over and watched a game, haven't we? For a bit of relaxation.

BEN: Things have tightened up, mate. They've tightened up.
    [GUS *chuckles to himself.*]

GUS: I saw the Villa get beat in a cup-tie once. Who was it against now? White shirts. It was one-all at half-time. I'll never forget it. Their opponents won by a penalty. Talk about drama. Yes, it was a disputed penalty. Disputed. They got beat two-one, anyway, because of it. You were there yourself.

BEN: Not me.

GUS: Yes, you were there. Don't you remember that disputed penalty?

BEN: No.

GUS: He went down just inside the area. Then they said he was just acting. I didn't think the other bloke touched him myself. But the referee had the ball on the spot.

BEN: Didn't touch him! What are you talking about? He laid him out flat!

GUS: Not the Villa. The Villa don't play that sort of game.

BEN: Get out of it.

[*Pause.*]

GUS: Eh, that must have been here, in Birmingham.

BEN: What must?

GUS: The Villa. That must have been here.

BEN: They were playing away.

GUS: Because you know who the other team was? It was the Spurs. It was Tottenham Hotspur.

BEN: Well, what about it?

GUS: We've never done a job in Tottenham.

BEN: How do you know?

GUS: I'd remember Tottenham.

[BEN *turns on his bed to look at him.*]

BEN: Don't make me laugh, will you?

[BEN *turns back and reads.* GUS *yawns and speaks through his yawn.*]

GUS: When's he going to get in touch? [*Pause.*] Yes, I'd like to see another football match. I've always been an ardent football fan. Here, what about coming to see the Spurs tomorrow?

BEN [*tonelessly*]: They're playing away.

GUS: Who are?

BEN: The Spurs.

GUS: Then they might be playing here.

BEN: Don't be silly.

GUS: If they're playing away they might be playing here. They might be playing the Villa.

BEN [*tonelessly*]: But the Villa are playing away.

[*Pause. An envelope slides under the door, right.* GUS *sees it. He stands, looking at it.*]

GUS: Ben.

BEN: Away. They're all playing away.

GUS: Ben, look here.

BEN: What?

GUS: Look.

94

[BEN *turns his head and sees the envelope. He stands.*]

BEN: What's that?

GUS: I don't know.

BEN: Where did it come from?

GUS: Under the door.

BEN: Well, what is it?

GUS: I don't know.

[*They stare at it.*]

BEN: Pick it up.

GUS: What do you mean?

BEN: Pick it up!

[GUS *slowly moves towards it, bends, and picks it up.*]

What is it?

GUS: An envelope.

BEN: Is there anything on it?

GUS: No.

BEN: Is it sealed?

GUS: Yes.

BEN: Open it.

GUS: What?

BEN: Open it!

[GUS *opens it and looks inside.*]

What's in it?

[GUS *empties twelve matches into his hand.*]

GUS: Matches.

BEN: Matches?

GUS: Yes.

BEN: Show it to me.

[GUS *passes the envelope.* BEN *examines it.*]

Nothing on it. Not a word.

GUS: That's funny, isn't it?

BEN: It came under the door?

GUS: Must have done.

BEN: Well, go on.

GUS: Go on where?

BEN: Open the door and see if you can catch anyone outside.

GUS: Who, me?

BEN: Go on!

[GUS *stares at him, puts the matches in his pocket, goes to his bed, and brings a revolver from under the pillow. He goes to the door, opens it, looks out, and shuts it.*]

GUS: No one. [*He replaces the revolver.*]

BEN: What did you see?

GUS: Nothing.

BEN: They must have been pretty quick.

[GUS *takes the matches from pocket and looks at them.*]

GUS: Well, they'll come in handy.

BEN: Yes.

GUS: Won't they?

BEN: Yes, you're always running out, aren't you?

GUS: All the time.

BEN: Well, they'll come in handy then.

GUS: Yes.

BEN: Won't they?

GUS: Yes, I could do with them. I could do with them too.

BEN: You could, eh?

GUS: Yes.

BEN: Why?

GUS: We haven't got any.

BEN: Well, you've got some now, haven't you?

GUS: I can light the kettle now.

BEN: Yes, you're always cadging matches. How many have you got there?

GUS: About a dozen.

BEN: Well, don't lose them. Red too. You don't even need a box.

[GUS *probes his ear with a match.*]

[*Slapping his hand*] Don't waste them! Go on, go and light it.

GUS: Eh?

BEN: Go and light it.

GUS: Light what?

BEN: The kettle.

GUS: You mean the gas.

BEN: Who does?

GUS: You do.

BEN [*his eyes narrowing*]: What do you mean, I mean the gas?

GUS: Well, that's what you mean, don't you? The gas.

BEN [*powerfully*]: If I say go and light the kettle I mean go and light the kettle.

GUS: How can you light a kettle?

BEN: It's a figure of speech! Light the kettle. It's a figure of speech!

GUS: I've never heard it.

BEN: Light the kettle! It's common usage!

GUS: I think you've got it wrong.

BEN [*menacing*]: What do you mean?

GUS: They say put on the kettle.

BEN [*taut*]: Who says?

[*They stare at each other, breathing hard.*]

[*Deliberately.*] I have never in all my life heard anyone say put on the kettle.

GUS: I bet my mother used to say it.

BEN: Your mother? When did you last see your mother?

GUS: I don't know, about –

BEN: Well, what are you talking about your mother for?

[*They stare.*]

Gus, I'm not trying to be unreasonable. I'm just trying to point out something to you.

GUS: Yes, but –

BEN: Who's the senior partner here, me or you?

GUS: You.

BEN: I'm only looking after your interests, Gus. You've got to learn, mate.

GUS: Yes, but I've never heard –

BEN [*vehemently*]: Nobody says light the gas! What does the gas light?

GUS: What does the gas –?

BEN [*grabbing him with two hands by the throat, at arm's length*]: THE KETTLE, YOU FOOL!

[*GUS takes the hands from his throat.*]

GUS: All right, all right.

[*Pause.*]

BEN: Well, what are you waiting for?

GUS: I want to see if they light.

BEN: What?

GUS: The matches. [*He takes out the flattened box and tries to strike.*] No. [*He throws the box under the bed.*]

[BEN *stares at him.* GUS *raises his foot.*]

Shall I try it on here?

[BEN *stares.* GUS *strikes a match on his shoe. It lights.*]

Here we are.

BEN [*wearily*]: Put on the bloody kettle, for Christ's sake. [BEN *goes to his bed, but realizing what he has said, stops and half turns. They look at each other.* GUS *slowly exits, left.* BEN *slams his paper down on the bed and sits on it, head in hands.*]

GUS [*entering*]: It's going.

BEN: What?

GUS: The stove. [GUS *goes to his bed and sits.*] I wonder who it'll be tonight.

[*Silence.*]

Eh, I've been wanting to ask you something.

BEN [*putting his legs on the bed*]: Oh, for Christ's sake.

GUS: No. I was going to ask you something. [*He rises and sits on* BEN'S *bed.*]

BEN: What are you sitting on my bed for?

[GUS *sits.*]

What's the matter with you? You're always asking me questions. What's the matter with you?

GUS: Nothing.

BEN: You never used to ask me so many damn questions. What's come over you?

GUS: No, I was just wondering.

BEN: Stop wondering. You've got a job to do. Why don't you just do it and shut up?

GUS: That's what I was wondering about.

BEN: What?

GUS: The job.

BEN: What job?

GUS [*tentatively*]: I thought perhaps you might know something.
[BEN *looks at him.*]
I thought perhaps you – I mean – have you got any idea – who it's going to be tonight?

BEN: Who what's going to be?
[*They look at each other.*]

GUS [*at length*]: Who it's going to be.
[*Silence.*]

BEN: Are you feeling all right?

GUS: Sure.

BEN: Go and make the tea.

GUS: Yes, sure. [GUS *exits, left,* BEN *looks after him. He then takes his revolver from under the pillow and checks it for ammunition.* GUS *re-enters.*] The gas has gone out.

BEN: Well, what about it?

GUS: There's a meter.

BEN: I haven't got any money.

GUS: Nor have I.

BEN: You'll have to wait.

GUS: What for?

BEN: For Wilson.

GUS: He might not come. He might just send a message. He doesn't always come.

BEN: Well, you'll have to do without it, won't you?

GUS: Blimey.

BEN: You'll have a cup of tea afterwards. What's the matter with you?

GUS: I like to have one before.
[BEN *holds the revolver up to the light and polishes it.*]

BEN: You'd better get ready anyway.

GUS: Well, I don't know, that's a bit much, you know, for my money. [*He picks up a packet of tea from the bed and throws it into the bag.*] I hope he's got a shilling, anyway, if he comes. He's entitled to have. After all, it's his place, he could have seen there was enough gas for a cup of tea.

BEN: What do you mean, it's his place?

GUS: Well, isn't it?

BEN: He's probably only rented it. It doesn't have to be his place.

GUS: I know it's his place. I bet the whole house is. He's not even laying on any gas now either. [GUS *sits on his bed.*] It's his place all right. Look at all the other places. You go to this address, there's a key there, there's a teapot, there's never a soul in sight – [*He pauses.*] Eh, nobody ever hears a thing, have you ever thought of that? We never get any complaints, do we, too much noise or anything like that? You never see a soul, do you? – except the bloke who comes. You ever noticed that? I wonder if the walls are sound-proof. [*He touches the wall above his bed.*] Can't tell. All you do is wait, eh? Half the time he doesn't even bother to put in an appearance, Wilson.

BEN: Why should he? He's a busy man.

GUS [*thoughtfully*]: I find him hard to talk to, Wilson. Do you know that, Ben?

BEN: Scrub round it, will you?

    [*Pause.*]

GUS: There are a number of things I want to ask him. But I can never get round to it, when I see him.

    [*Pause.*]

I've been thinking about the last one.

BEN: What last one?

GUS: That girl.

    [BEN *grabs the paper, which he reads.*]

    [*Rising, looking down at Ben.*] How many times have you read that paper?

    [BEN *slams the paper down and rises.*]

BEN [*angrily*]: What do you mean?

GUS: I was just wondering how many times you'd –

BEN: What are you doing, criticizing me?

GUS: No, I was just –

BEN: You'll get a swipe round your earhole if you don't watch your step.

GUS: Now look here, Ben –

BEN: I'm not looking anywhere! [*He addresses the room.*] How many times have I –? A bloody liberty!

GUS: I didn't mean that.

BEN: You just get on with it, mate. Get on with it, that's all. [BEN *gets back on the bed.*]

GUS: I was just thinking about that girl, that's all. [GUS *sits on his bed.*] She wasn't much to look at, I know, but still. It was a mess though, wasn't it? What a mess. Honest, I can't remember a mess like that one. They don't seem to hold together like men, women. A looser texture, like. Didn't she spread, eh? She didn't half spread. Kaw! But I've been meaning to ask you.

[BEN *sits up and clenches his eyes.*]

Who clears up after we've gone? I'm curious about that. Who does the clearing up? Maybe they don't clear up. Maybe they just leave them there, eh? What do you think? How many jobs have we done? Blimey, I can't count them. What if they never clear anything up after we've gone?

BEN [*pityingly*]: You mutt. Do you think we're the only branch of this organization? Have a bit of common. They got departments for everything.

GUS: What cleaners and all?

BEN: You birk!

GUS: No, it was that girl made me start to think –

[*There is a loud clatter and racket in the bulge of wall between the beds, of something descending. They grab their revolvers, jump up, and face the wall. The noise comes to a stop. Silence. They look at each other.* BEN *gestures sharply towards the wall.* GUS *approaches the wall slowly. He bangs it with his revolver. It is hollow.* BEN *moves to the head of his bed, his revolver cocked.* GUS *puts his revolver on his bed and pats along the bottom of the centre panel. He finds a rim. He lifts the panel. Disclosed is a serving-hatch, a 'dumb waiter'. A wide box is held by pulleys.* GUS *peers into the box. He brings out a piece of paper.*]

BEN: What is it?

GUS: You have a look at it.

BEN: Read it.

GUS [*reading*]: Two braised steak and chips. Two sago puddings. Two teas without sugar.

BEN: Let me see that. [*He takes the paper.*]

GUS [*to himself*]: Two teas without sugar.

BEN: Mmnn.

GUS: What do you think of that?

BEN: Well –

[*The box goes up.* BEN *levels his revolver.*]

GUS: Give us a chance! They're in a hurry, aren't they?

[BEN *re-reads the note.* GUS *looks over his shoulder.*]

That's a bit – that's a bit funny, isn't it?

BEN [*quickly*]: No. It's not funny. It probably used to be a café here, that's all. Upstairs. These places change hands very quickly.

GUS: A café?

BEN: Yes.

GUS: What, you mean this was the kitchen, down here?

BEN: Yes, they change hands overnight, these places. Go into liquidation. The people who run it, you know, they don't find it a going concern, they move out.

GUS: You mean the people who ran this place didn't find it a going concern and moved out?

BEN: Sure.

GUS: WELL, WHO'S GOT IT NOW?

[*Silence.*]

BEN: What do you mean, who's got it now?

GUS: Who's got it now? If they moved out, who moved in?

BEN: Well, that all depends –

[*The box descends with a clatter and bang.* BEN *levels his revolver.* GUS *goes to the box and brings out a piece of paper.*]

GUS [*reading*]: Soup of the day. Liver and onions. Jam tart.

[*A pause.* GUS *looks at Ben.* BEN *takes the note and reads it. He walks slowly to the hatch.* GUS *follows.* BEN *looks into the hatch but not up it.* GUS *puts his hand on Ben's shoulder.* BEN *throws it off.* GUS *puts his finger to his mouth. He leans on the hatch and swiftly looks up it.* BEN *flings him away in alarm.* BEN *looks at the note. He throws his revolver on the bed and speaks with decision.*]

BEN: We'd better send something up.

GUS: Eh?

BEN: We'd better send something up.

GUS: Oh! Yes. Yes. Maybe you're right.

[*They are both relieved at the decision.*]

BEN [*purposefully*]: Quick! What have you got in that bag?

GUS: Not much. [GUS *goes to the hatch and shouts up it.*] Wait a minute.

BEN: Don't do that!

[GUS *examines the contents of the bag and brings them out, one by one.*]

GUS: Biscuits. A bar of chocolate. Half a pint of milk.

BEN: That all?

GUS: Packet of tea.

BEN: Good.

GUS: We can't send the tea. That's all the tea we've got.

BEN: Well, there's no gas. You can't do anything with it, can you?

GUS: Maybe they can send us down a bob.

BEN: What else is there?

GUS [*reaching into bag*]: One Eccles cake.

BEN: One Eccles cake?

GUS: Yes.

BEN: You never told me you had an Eccles cake.

GUS: Didn't I?

BEN: Why only one? Didn't you bring one for me?

GUS: I didn't think you'd be keen.

BEN: Well, you can't send up one Eccles cake, anyway.

GUS: Why not?

BEN: Fetch one of those plates.

GUS: All right. [GUS *goes towards the door, left, and stops.*] Do you mean I can keep the Eccles cake then?

BEN: Keep it?

GUS: Well, they don't know we've got it, do they?

BEN: That's not the point.

GUS: Can't I keep it?

BEN: No, you can't. Get the plate.

[GUS *exits, left.* BEN *looks in the bag. He brings out a packet of crisps. Enter* GUS *with a plate.*]

[*Accusingly, holding up the crisps.*] Where did these come from?

GUS: What?

BEN: Where did these crisps come from?

GUS: Where did you find them?

BEN [*hitting him on the shoulder*]: You're playing a dirty game, my lad!

GUS: I only eat those with beer!

BEN: Well, where were you going to get the beer?

GUS: I was saving them till I did.

BEN: I'll remember this. Put everything on the plate.

[*They pile everything on to the plate. The box goes up without the plate.*]

Wait a minute!

[*They stand.*]

GUS: It's gone up.

BEN: It's all your stupid fault, playing about!

GUS: What do we do now?

BEN: We'll have to wait till it comes down. [BEN *puts the plate on the bed, puts on his shoulder holster, and starts to put on his tie.*] You'd better get ready.

[GUS *goes to his bed, puts on his tie, and starts to fix his holster.*]

GUS: Hey, Ben.

BEN: What?

GUS: What's going on here?

[*Pause.*]

BEN: What do you mean?

GUS: How can this be a café?

BEN: It used to be a café.

GUS: Have you seen the gas stove?

BEN: What about it?

GUS: It's only got three rings.

BEN: So what?

GUS: Well, you couldn't cook much on three rings, not for a busy place like this.

BEN [*irritably*]: That's why the service is slow! [BEN *puts on his waist-coat.*]

GUS: Yes, but what happens when we're not here? What do they do then? All these menus coming down and nothing going up. It might have been going on like this for years.

[BEN *brushes his jacket.*]

What happens when we go?

[BEN *puts on his jacket.*]

They can't do much business.

[*The box descends. They turn about.* GUS *goes to the hatch and brings out a note.*]

GUS [*reading*]: Macaroni Pastitsio. Ormitha Macarounada.

BEN: What was that?

GUS: Macaroni Pastitsio. Ormitha Macarounada.

BEN: Greek dishes.

GUS: No.

BEN: That's right.

GUS: That's pretty high class.

BEN: Quick before it goes up.

[GUS *puts the plate in the box.*]

GUS [*calling up the hatch*]: Three McVitie and Price! One Lyons Red Label! One Smith's Crisps! One Eccles cake! One Fruit and Nut!

BEN: Cadbury's.

GUS [*up the hatch*]: Cadbury's!

BEN [*handing the milk*]: One bottle of milk.

GUS [*up the hatch*]: One bottle of milk! Half a pint! [*He looks at the label.*] Express Dairy! [*He puts the bottle in the box.*]

[*The box goes up.*]

Just did it.

BEN: You shouldn't shout like that.

GUS: Why not?

BEN: It isn't done. [BEN *goes to his bed.*] Well, that should be all right, anyway, for the time being.

GUS: You think so, eh?

BEN: Get dressed, will you? It'll be any minute now.

[GUS *puts on his waistcoat.* BEN *lies down and looks up at the ceiling.*]

GUS: This is some place. No tea and no biscuits.

BEN: Eating makes you lazy, mate. You're getting lazy, you know that? You don't want to get slack on your job.

GUS: Who me?

BEN: Slack, mate, slack.

GUS: Who me? Slack?

BEN: Have you checked your gun? You haven't even checked your gun. It looks disgraceful, anyway. Why don't you ever polish it?

[GUS *rubs his revolver on the sheet.* BEN *takes out a pocket mirror and straightens his tie.*]

GUS: I wonder where the cook is. They must have had a few, to cope with that. Maybe they had a few more gas stoves. Eh! Maybe there's another kitchen along the passage.

BEN: Of course there is! Do you know what it takes to make an Ormitha Macarounada?

GUS: No, what?

BEN: An Ormitha –! Buck your ideas up, will you?

GUS: Takes a few cooks, eh? [GUS *puts his revolver in its holster.*] The sooner we're out of this place the better. [*He puts on his jacket.*] Why doesn't he get in touch? I feel like I've been here years. [*He takes his revolver out of its holster to check the ammunition.*] We've never let him down though, have we? We've never let him down. I was thinking only the other day, Ben. We're reliable, aren't we? [*He puts his revolver back in its holster.*] Still, I'll be glad when it's over tonight. [*He brushes his jacket.*] I hope the bloke's not going to get excited tonight, or anything. I'm feeling a bit off. I've got a splitting headache.

[*Silence.*]

[*The box descends.* BEN *jumps up.* GUS *collects the note.*]

[*Reading.*] One Bamboo Shoots, Water Chestnuts, and Chicken. One Char Siu and Beansprouts.

BEN: Beansprouts?

GUS: Yes.

BEN: Blimey.

GUS: I wouldn't know where to begin. [*He looks back at the box. The packet of tea is inside it. He picks it up.*] They've sent back the tea.

BEN [*anxious*]: What'd they do that for?

GUS: Maybe it isn't tea time.

[*The box goes up. Silence.*]

BEN [*throwing the tea on the bed, and speaking urgently*]: Look here. We'd better tell them.

GUS: Tell them what?

BEN: That we can't do it, we haven't got it.

GUS: All right then.

BEN: Lend us your pencil. We'll write a note.

[GUS, *turning for a pencil, suddenly discovers the speaking-tube, which hangs on the right wall of the hatch facing his bed.*]

GUS: What's this?

BEN: What?

GUS: This.

BEN [*examining it*]: This? It's a speaking-tube.

GUS: How long has that been there?

BEN: Just the job. We should have used it before, instead of shouting up there.

GUS: Funny I never noticed it before.

BEN: Well, come on.

GUS: What do you do?

BEN: See that? That's a whistle.

GUS: What, this?

BEN: Yes, take it out. Pull it out.

[GUS *does so.*]

That's it.

GUS: What do we do now?

BEN: Blow into it.

GUS: Blow?

BEN: It whistles up there if you blow. Then they know you want to speak. Blow.

[GUS *blows. Silence.*]

GUS [*tube at mouth*]: I can't hear a thing.

BEN: Now you speak! Speak into it!

[GUS *looks at Ben, then speaks into the tube.*]

GUS: The larder's bare!

BEN: Give me that! [*He grabs the tube and puts it to his mouth. Speaking with great deference.*] Good evening, I'm sorry to – bother you, but we just thought we'd better let you know that we haven't got anything left. We sent up all we had. There's no more food down here. [*He brings the tube slowly to his ear.*] What? [*To mouth.*] What? [*To ear. He listens. To mouth.*] No, all we had we sent up. [*To ear. He listens. To mouth.*] Oh, I'm very sorry to hear that. [*To ear. He listens. To Gus.*] The Eccles cake was stale. [*He listens. To Gus*] The chocolate was melted. [*He listens. To Gus.*] The milk was sour.

GUS: What about the crisps?

BEN [*listening*]: The biscuits were mouldy. [*He glares at Gus. Tube to mouth.*] Well, we're very sorry about that. [*Tube to ear.*] What? [*To mouth.*] What? [*To ear.*] Yes. Yes. [*To mouth.*] Yes certainly. Certainly. Right away. [*To ear. The voice has ceased. He hangs up the tube. Excitedly.*] Did you hear that?

GUS: What?

BEN: You know what he said? Light the kettle! Not put on the kettle! Not light the gas! But light the kettle!

GUS: How can we light the kettle?

BEN: What do you mean?

GUS: There's no gas.

BEN [*clapping hand to head*]: Now what do we do?

GUS: What did he want us to light the kettle for?

BEN: For tea. He wanted a cup of tea.

GUS: *He* wanted a cup of tea! What about me? I've been wanting a cup of tea all night!

BEN [*despairingly*]: What do we do now?

GUS: What are we supposed to drink?

[BEN *sits on his bed, staring.*]

What about us?

[BEN *sits.*]

I'm thirsty too. I'm starving. And he wants a cup of tea. That beats the band that does.

[BEN *lets his head sink on to his chest.*]

I could do with a bit of sustenance myself. What about you? You look as if you could do with something too. [GUS *sits on his bed.*] We send him up all we've got and he's not satisfied. No, honest, it's enough to make the cat laugh. Why did you send him up all that stuff? [*Thoughtfully*] Why did I send it up?

[*Pause.*]

Who knows what he's got upstairs? He's probably got a salad bowl. They must have something up there. They won't get much from down here. You notice they didn't ask for any salads? They've probably got a salad bowl up there. Cold meat, radishes, cucumbers. Watercress. Roll mops.

[*Pause.*]

Hardboiled eggs.

[*Pause.*]

The lot. They've probably got a crate of beer too. Probably eating my crisps with a pint of beer now. Didn't have anything to say about those crisps, did he? They do all right, don't worry about that. You don't think they're just going to sit there and wait for stuff to come up from down here, do you? That'll get them nowhere.

[*Pause.*]

They do all right.

[*Pause.*]

And he wants a cup of tea.

[*Pause.*]

That's past a joke, in my opinion. [*He looks over at Ben, rises, and goes to him.*] What's the matter with you? You don't look too bright. I feel like an Alka-Seltzer myself.

[BEN *sits up.*]

BEN [*in a low voice*]: Time's getting on.

GUS: I know. I don't like doing a job on an empty stomach.

BEN [*wearily*]: Be quiet a minute. Let me give you your instructions.

GUS: What for? We always do it the same way, don't we?

BEN: Let me give you your instructions.

[GUS *sighs and sits next to Ben on the bed. The instructions are stated and repeated automatically.*]

When we get the call, you go over and stand behind the door.

GUS: Stand behind the door.

BEN: If there's a knock on the door you don't answer it.

GUS: If there's a knock on the door I don't answer it.

BEN: But there won't be a knock on the door.

GUS: So I won't answer it.

BEN: When the bloke comes in –

GUS: When the bloke comes in –

BEN: Shut the door behind him.

GUS: Shut the door behind him.

BEN: Without divulging your presence.

GUS: Without divulging my presence.

BEN: He'll see me and come towards me.

GUS: He'll see you and come towards you.

BEN: He won't see you.

GUS [absently]: Eh?

BEN: He won't see you.

GUS: He won't see me.

BEN: But he'll see me.

GUS: He'll see you.

BEN: He won't know you're there.

GUS: He won't know you're there.

BEN: He won't know *you're* there.

GUS: He won't know I'm there.

BEN: I take out my gun.

GUS: You take out your gun.

BEN: He stops in his tracks.

GUS: He stops in his tracks.

BEN: If he turns round –

GUS: If he turns round –

BEN: You're there.

GUS: I'm here.

[BEN *frowns and presses his forehead.*]

You've missed something out.

BEN: I know. What?

GUS: I haven't taken my gun out, according to you.

BEN: You take your gun out –

GUS: After I've closed the door.

BEN: After you've closed the door.

GUS: You've never missed that out before, you know that?

BEN: When he sees you behind him –

GUS: Me behind him –

BEN: And me in front of him –

GUS: And you in front of him –

BEN: He'll feel uncertain –

GUS: Uneasy.

BEN: He won't know what to do.

GUS: So what will he do?

BEN: He'll look at me and he'll look at you.

GUS: We won't say a word.

BEN: We'll look at him.

GUS: He won't say a word.

BEN: He'll look at us.

GUS: And we'll look at him.

BEN: Nobody says a word.

[*Pause.*]

GUS: What do we do if it's a girl?

BEN: We do the same.

GUS: Exactly the same?

BEN: Exactly.

[*Pause.*]

GUS: We don't do anything different?

BEN: We do exactly the same.

GUS: Oh. [GUS *rises, and shivers.*] Excuse me.

[*He exits through the door on the left.* BEN *remains sitting on the bed, still. The lavatory chain is pulled once off left, but the lavatory does not flush.*]

[*Silence.*]

[GUS *re-enters and stops inside the door, deep in thought. He looks at Ben, then walks slowly across to his own bed. He is troubled. He stands, thinking. He turns and looks at Ben. He moves a few paces towards him.*]

[*Slowly in a low, tense voice.*] Why did he send us matches if he knew there was no gas?

[*Silence.*]

[BEN *stares in front of him.* GUS *crosses to the left side of Ben to the foot of his bed, to get to his other ear.*]

Ben. Why did he send us matches if he knew there was no gas?

[BEN *looks up*.]

Why did he do that?

BEN: Who?

GUS: Who sent us those matches?

BEN: What are you talking about?

♠   [GUS *stares down at him*.]

GUS [*thickly*]: Who is it upstairs?

BEN [*nervously*]: What's one thing to do with another?

GUS: Who is it, though?

BEN: What's one thing to do with another? [BEN *fumbles for his paper on the bed*.]

GUS: I asked you a question.

BEN: Enough!

GUS [*with growing agitation*]: I asked you before. Who moved in? I asked you. You said the people who had it before moved out. Well, who moved in?

BEN [*hunched*]: Shut up.

GUS: I told you, didn't I?

BEN [*standing*]: Shut up!

GUS [*feverishly*]: I told you before who owned this place, didn't I? I told you.

[BEN *hits him viciously on the shoulder*.]

I told you who ran this place, didn't I?

[BEN *hits him viciously on the shoulder*.]

[*Violently*.] Well, what's he playing all these games for? That's what I want to know. What's he doing it for?

BEN: What games?

GUS [*passionately, advancing*]: What's he doing it for? We've been through our tests, haven't we? We got right through our tests, years ago, didn't we? We took them together, don't you remember, didn't we? We've proved ourselves before now, haven't we? We've always done our job. What's he doing all this for? What's the idea? What's he playing these games for?

[*The box in the shaft comes down behind them. The noise is this time accompanied by a shrill whistle, as it falls.* GUS *rushes to the hatch and seizes the note.*]

[*Reading*] Scampi!

[*He crumples the note, picks up the tube, takes out the whistle, blows, and speaks.*]

WE'VE GOT NOTHING LEFT! NOTHING! DO YOU UNDERSTAND?

[BEN *seizes the tube and flings Gus away. He follows Gus and slaps him hard, back-handed, across the chest.*]

BEN: Stop it! You maniac!

GUS: But you heard!

BEN [*savagely*]: That's enough! I'm warning you!

[*Silence.*]

[BEN *hangs the tube. He goes to his bed and lies down. He picks up his paper and reads.*]

[*Silence.*]

[*The box goes up. They turn quickly, their eyes meet.* BEN *turns to his paper. Slowly* GUS *goes back to his bed, and sits.*]

[*Silence.*]

[*The hatch falls back into place. They turn quickly, their eyes meet.* BEN *turns back to his paper.*]

[*Silence.*]

[BEN *throws his paper down.*]

BEN: Kaw!

[*He picks up the paper and looks at it.*]

Listen to this!

[*Pause.*]

What about that, eh?

[*Pause.*]

Kaw!

[*Pause.*]

Have you ever heard such a thing?

GUS [*dully*]: Go on!

BEN: It's true.

GUS: Get away.

BEN: It's down here in black and white.

GUS [*very low*]: Is that a fact?

BEN: Can you imagine it?

GUS: It's unbelievable.

BEN: It's enough to make you want to puke, isn't it?

GUS [*almost inaudible*]: Incredible.

[BEN *shakes his head. He puts the paper down and rises. He fixes the revolver in his holster.* GUS *stands up. He goes to the door on the left.*]

BEN: Where are you going?

GUS: I'm going to have a glass of water.

[*He exits.* BEN *brushes dust off his clothes and shoes. The whistle in the speaking-tube blows. He goes to it, takes the whistle out and puts the tube to his ear. He listens. He puts it to his mouth.*]

BEN: Yes. [*To ear. He listens. To mouth.*] Straight away. Right. [*To ear. He listens. To mouth.*] Sure we're ready. [*To ear. He listens. To mouth.*] Understood. Repeat. He has arrived and will be coming in straight away. The normal method to be employed. Understood. [*To ear. He listens. To mouth.*] Sure we're ready. [*To ear. He listens. To mouth.*] Right. [*He hangs the tube up.*] Gus! [*He takes out a comb and combs his hair, adjusts his jacket to diminish the bulge of the revolver. The lavatory flushes off left.* BEN *goes quickly to the door, left.*] Gus!

[*The door right opens sharply.* BEN *turns, his revolver levelled at the door.* GUS *stumbles in. He is stripped of his jacket, waistcoat, tie, holster, and revolver. He stops, body stooping, his arms at his sides. He raises his head and looks at Ben. A long silence. They stare at each other.*]

CURTAIN

N. F. SIMPSON

A Resounding Tinkle

A RESOUNDING TINKLE

First presented in a shortened and rearranged version by The English Stage Society, at The Royal Court Theatre, London, on 1 December 1957, with the following cast:

FIRST COMEDIAN	Graham Crowden
SECOND COMEDIAN	Toke Townley
TECHNICIAN	Leslie Glazer
PRODUCER	Patrick Barton
FIRST CLEANER	Rita Webb
SECOND CLEANER	Fanny Carby
BRO PARADOCK	Nigel Davenport
MIDDIE PARADOCK	Wendy Craig
UNCLE TED	Marigold Sharman
AUTHOR	John Wood

Directed by William Gaskill

SCENE: A surburban living room
TIME: The present

CHARACTERS OF THE PLAY

BRO PARADOCK
MIDDIE PARADOCK, *his wife*
FIRST COMEDIAN, *Hamster*
SECOND COMEDIAN, *Bug*
TECHNICIAN
AUTHOR
MRS NORA MORTICE, *a neighbour*
FIRST CLEANER
SECOND CLEANER
DON PARADOCK, *daughter of Bro and Middie Paradock*
MUSTARD SHORT ⎫
DENZIL PEPPER ⎪
MISS SALT   ⎬ *critics*
MRS VINEGAR   ⎪
CHAIRMAN   ⎭
MAN IN BOWLER HAT
PRODUCER

ACT ONE

SCENE 1

A suburban living room. Evening.

[*The silence between* BRO PARADOCK, *who stands with a glass in his hand looking out of the window, and his wife,* MIDDIE PARA-DOCK, *whose glass stands beside her on the small table by which she is sitting, has clearly just fallen. It is not broken for nearly half a minute.*]

MRS PARADOCK: So don't flatter yourself.

[BRO PARADOCK *turns from the window, empties his glass, and, picking up Middie Paradock's glass, goes to a side table to fill both from one of two bottles containing a brightly purple liquid.*]

MR PARADOCK: I'm not flattering myself. And in any case we had all this out before.

MRS PARADOCK: And now we're having it out again.

[BRO PARADOCK *hands one of the two glasses to his wife. Both raise their glasses perfunctorily, grunt, and sip. They are far from certain what to make of the bliss they come upon for the second time, and* BRO PARADOCK, *after another two sips, takes up the bottle and looks steadily at the label.*]

MR PARADOCK: I've never known this to happen before.

MRS PARADOCK: It doesn't have to have happened before.

MR PARADOCK: I can feel it hurrying through my veins like smoke.

MRS PARADOCK: It's happened now. That's all you need concern yourself with.

MR PARADOCK: My lines seem to be coming to me in bits. Or what seem to be bits. This is like some unspecified milk of paradise.

MRS PARADOCK: What you can't remember you can make up.

MR PARADOCK: And what I can't make up can go unsaid.

MRS PARADOCK: No one minds with this kind of play. No one notices. You can be eight sheets in the wind or whatever it is practically from the word Go and the more the merrier from the author down. Or up. So don't for God's sake start having any qualms over remembering your lines or anybody else's lines. Just put it down to the ambrosia. Let ambrosia look after it.

MR PARADOCK: Ambrosia is what they eat. Not what they drink.

MRS PARADOCK: What who eat?

MR PARADOCK: You mean nectar. Let the nectar look after it. Not ambrosia.

MRS PARADOCK: Who said anything about nectar?

MR PARADOCK: You can't *drink* ambrosia for God's sake! Ambrosia is the food of the immortals. It's what the gods eat.

MRS PARADOCK: I don't know what it is you're trying to prove with your slick emendations of every damn remark I make, but whatever it is you can go right ahead and prove something different.

[*A knock.*]

MRS PARADOCK [*going out to answer the knock*]: What the hell do you think you make me look like by comparison?

[BRO PARADOCK *takes up a newspaper.* MIDDIE PARADOCK *returns and begins tidying the room, speaking as she does so.*]

MRS PARADOCK: There's somebody at the door wanting you to form a government.

[BRO PARADOCK *looks at her in astonishment. Several seconds elapse.*]

MR PARADOCK: What does he look like?

MRS PARADOCK: He says he's working through the street directory.

[*Pause.*]

MRS PARADOCK: I shall want this cork opened in case we have to offer him a drink. [*Pause.*] He was wearing an old raincoat. He looked as if he was trying it on for size.

MR PARADOCK: Give me the bottle. You can't open a cork. You should know that. You open the bottle [*He begins to remove the cork.*] If it's an old raincoat what would he be trying it on for?

MRS PARADOCK: It might not be as old as the one he had before.

MR PARADOCK: I don't know why you wanted this bottle opened when the other one's more than half full.

MRS PARADOCK: The coat he had before may have been in tatters. It may have been black with grease. Or mud.

[*With a preoccupied air* BRO PARADOCK *takes a pipe from the mantelpiece and begins filling it.*]

MR PARADOCK: How can I start forming a government at six o'clock in the evening?

MRS PARADOCK: You'd be saying the same thing if it were six o'clock in the morning. [*She takes a torn and dirty raincoat from a cupboard.*] Look at this thing. How do you know his mightn't have been in a worse state than this one? Look at the sleeves. And the collar – look at it. His was probably as bad or worse.

MR PARADOCK: It's the Prime Minister's job.

MRS PARADOCK: Oh yes. If you want to shelve your responsibilities I dare say it is the Prime Minister's job.

MR PARADOCK: It's no concern of mine at all.

MRS PARADOCK: There's a man at the door waiting for your answer. [*Pause.*]

MR PARADOCK: How do you know he isn't wanted by the police?

MRS PARADOCK: Why should he be?

MR PARADOCK: If he is we ought to turn him over.

MRS PARADOCK: If he's a criminal, he's in plain clothes – that's all I can say.

MR PARADOCK: I'm going to turn him over. [*He moves to the door.*]

MRS PARADOCK: You may never get another chance to form a government.

MR PARADOCK: That goes for anything I ever choose not to do.

MRS PARADOCK: So what's it to be?

MR PARADOCK: I'll see what he looks like.

[*He goes out.* MIDDIE PARADOCK *clears the table, sets out paper, ashtrays, water, and glasses as for a board meeting.* BRO PARADOCK *returns, takes up a newspaper, and sits down in silence. Pause.*]

MR PARADOCK: It was Uncle Ted having a joke.

MRS PARADOCK: I would have recognized him.

MR PARADOCK: He was disguising his voice. He said I looked like Gladstone.

MRS PARADOCK: And did you?

MR PARADOCK: He wanted me to be taken in – I could see that.

MRS PARADOCK: So I suppose you obliged?

MR PARADOCK: That sort of thing cuts no ice with me.

MRS PARADOCK: You should have led him on by pretending to think it was 1868.

MR PARADOCK: It was all of a piece with his asking me to form a government.

MRS PARADOCK: I hope you didn't start saying: My mission is to pacify Ireland?

MR PARADOCK: It cut no more ice with me than Gladstone would have done if I'd been Queen Victoria. And God knows there's little enough of the Empress of India about me.

MRS PARADOCK: It would have been playing into his hands to say: My mission is to pacify Ireland.

MR PARADOCK: I know it would have been playing into his hands.

MRS PARADOCK: I can't think why I didn't recognize him.

MR PARADOCK: He said he was round canvassing for the Whigs.

MRS PARADOCK: Surely Uncle Ted knows you've never been a Whig?

MR PARADOCK: I suppose he thought he could talk me round like last time, when he had me voting for some candidate who refused to stand.

MRS PARADOCK: You should have let him come in for a few minutes to try your overcoat on.

MR PARADOCK: My overcoat would never fit Uncle Ted. Uncle Ted is broader across the shoulders than I am.

MRS PARADOCK: Exactly.

MR PARADOCK: He's a bigger man altogether than I am. He'd never get into my overcoat. I doubt whether he could even wear it like a cloak.

MRS PARADOCK: You don't see what I'm leading up to, do you? I know your overcoat is too small for him. It's too small for you except when you're in one of your pint-size moods. But if he'd tried it on I could have seen at a glance he wasn't a man of your build. I might after a time have been able to narrow it down to Uncle Ted. As it is I don't know what to think.

MR PARADOCK: I've already told you it was Uncle Ted having a joke with us. It's just the kind of joke Uncle Ted would think up.

MRS PARADOCK: And what happened about the government? Did you agree to form one or not?

MR PARADOCK: I wasn't approached.

MRS PARADOCK: That's a likely story.

MR PARADOCK: He probably forgot.

MRS PARADOCK: If he forgot how do you know it was Uncle Ted? It looks to me as if you've let yourself in for something with your bland assumptions about it being Uncle Ted having a joke with us. You'll be getting somebody round before you know where you are with papers to prove it's 1868.

MR PARADOCK: But not that I'm Gladstone.

MRS PARADOCK: If it's 1868 it makes precious little difference whether you're Gladstone or Disraeli.

[*A knock.*]

MR PARADOCK: Tell them I'm in conference.

MRS PARADOCK: It'll be the concert party I expect.

[MIDDIE PARADOCK *goes out.* BRO PARADOCK *sits down at the head of the table as though presiding at a directors' meeting of four, whose names around the table anti-clockwise from himself are Black, Green, White, and Brown.* BRO PARADOCK *appears to be following a discussion which is passing back and forth across the table. Occasionally he intervenes to clarify a point, to invite a comment or to call someone to order.* MIDDIE PARADOCK *returns.*]

MRS PARADOCK: I've sent them upstairs to get their make-up on. It's the concert party.

MR PARADOCK: Where are they going to do their act? There's no room in here for them.

MRS PARADOCK: It doesn't last more than ten minutes or so.

MR PARADOCK: They've still got to have somewhere to do it.

MRS PARADOCK: They can do it in the room next door. We can watch through the serving hatch there. We've done it before.

MR PARADOCK [*shrugs*]: As long as they're satisfied. Give me a hand to get this board meeting out of the way before they come down, Middie.

MRS PARADOCK: If I can find my shorthand.

[MIDDIE PARADOCK *fetches a notebook and pencil, quickly tidies*

her hair as she passes a mirror, puts on stylishly elegant spectacles, and
sits down beside Bro Paradock. The mime continues for a few moments,
and BRO PARADOCK *then rises to close the meeting.*]

MR PARADOCK: Gentlemen. We have several proposals before us. I
think we have three, to be exact – unless Mr Black's last point is
to be taken as expanding the total to three and a half! [*He acknow-*
ledges laughter.] The question is whether by continuing the meeting
for another three or four hours we can reduce those three – and a
half – proposals to one, or whether it would be better to congratu-
late ourselves on the progress we have already made and postpone
a final decision for later consideration. As you know, gentlemen,
and it is a melancholy thought – whatever we may decide, whatever plans we may make for the future of the company, it is beyond
any of us to predict the conditions under which those plans will
have to work, since no one can forecast – and perhaps least of all
the government itself, what the government's future policy towards
typewriter ribbons is to be. [*He acknowledges laughter.*] We have
cleared a great deal of useful ground here this afternoon, and I
think you will agree with me when I say . . .

[FIRST COMEDIAN, *wearing a white coat and carrying a stethoscope,*
enters.]

MRS PARADOCK: Here they are.

FIRST COMEDIAN: The other one's coming in a moment. Where
would you like us?

MRS PARADOCK [*opening the door, right, into an adjoining room*]: We
thought perhaps in here would be rather nice.

[MIDDIE PARADOCK *leads* FIRST COMEDIAN *out, switching on*
the light to reveal a small adjoining room containing a wash-basin, a
light, long wooden table, and a desk. BRO PARADOCK *puts his head*
through the hatch.]

MRS PARADOCK: We haven't got a stage for you I'm afraid, but
there's any amount of hot water upstairs if you want to wash the
make-up off afterwards.

MR PARADOCK: We thought for the moment you were Uncle Ted
back.

MRS PARADOCK: We thought nothing of the kind. He thinks it's

1868 and you've come to ask him to form a government. It's all he ever thinks about.

FIRST COMEDIAN: I'd like an old blanket on this table, Mrs Paradock, and two or three cushions if you could manage it.

MRS PARADOCK: I can manage the blanket; I'll see what I can find for you to use as cushions.

FIRST COMEDIAN: A pillow would do. I only want to prop his head up.

MRS PARADOCK: I'll find something. And say nothing to him whatever you do about Edward Cardwell. He's only waiting for a chance to have you reforming the Army. He thinks he's Gladstone.

MR PARADOCK: I'm not deaf and I don't need humouring, thank you.

MRS PARADOCK: Cushions and a blanket.

[MIDDIE PARADOCK *goes out.*]

MR PARADOCK: There's plenty of hot water in the bathroom upstairs.

[FIRST COMEDIAN *continues in silence to set his scene, placing the table near the front of the stage and arranging papers on the desk.* MIDDIE PARADOCK *comes in with blanket and cushions.*]

MR PARADOCK: I was telling our friend here there's plenty of hot water upstairs if they want it afterwards.

MRS PARADOCK: A spotlight would be more to the point. They can't do their act in total darkness.

MR PARADOCK: It isn't what they can do that matters. Or what they can't do. It's what we can see them doing. That's the thing that matters.

FIRST COMEDIAN [*placing cushions under the blanket with which he covers the table to form an improvised couch as for a doctor's patient*]: I think we're about ready now if you wouldn't mind giving my friend a shout. He can come through the same door there when you've put out the light in your room.

MRS PARADOCK: Do you hear that, Bro? We're to have our light out. You'd better have your torch ready.

[MIDDIE PARADOCK *goes out and returns almost immediately.*]

MRS PARADOCK: He's just coming down. Where's your torch, Bro
before I switch out the light?

MR PARADOCK: It's here ready. I've had it ready all the time while
you've been talking.

MRS PARADOCK: Isn't this exciting?

[*She switches off the light. By the light of the torch she finds her way
to the hatch.* FIRST COMEDIAN *is sitting at his improvised desk
writing. He leans forward, presses a button, and says* 'Ping'. *The door
from the living room opens to admit a man of no particular age between
forty and sixty, whose nondescript appearance and defeated air contrast
with the brisk ebullient manner the First Comedian has assumed.
This is the* SECOND COMEDIAN. *He approaches the desk and sits
diffidently down. When after a few minutes the* FIRST COMEDIAN
disengages his attention from what he is writing, the SECOND
COMEDIAN *leans forward.*]

SECOND COMEDIAN: It's my feet, Doctor.

FIRST COMEDIAN: What's the matter with your feet?

SECOND COMEDIAN: I was rather hoping you might be able to tell
me that, Doctor.

FIRST COMEDIAN: Let me see them.

[SECOND COMEDIAN *takes off shoes and socks.*]

SECOND COMEDIAN: They're all right now. It's when they suddenly
swivel round they catch me.

[SECOND COMEDIAN *holds out both legs quite straight in front of
him.* FIRST COMEDIAN *stands over them.*]

FIRST COMEDIAN: What are these?

SECOND COMEDIAN: They're my kneecaps, Doctor.

FIRST COMEDIAN: They ought to be much higher up your legs than
this.

SECOND COMEDIAN: I can't seem to keep them up, Doctor.

FIRST COMEDIAN: Take everything off except your trousers and lie
down over there.

[FIRST COMEDIAN *goes to wash-basin where he begins washing his
hands, while* SECOND COMEDIAN *goes into the corner, where the
desk conceals him, to undress.*]

FIRST COMEDIAN: Eardrums still getting overheated?

SECOND COMEDIAN: Only when I listen to anything, Doctor.

[SECOND COMEDIAN *comes out and lies down on the couch.* FIRST COMEDIAN *examines his chest.*]

FIRST COMEDIAN: Breathe in deeply. Again. Yes – you're having trouble with your breathing. Breathe out. Do you notice any difference?

SECOND COMEDIAN: None at all, Doctor.

FIRST COMEDIAN: And do you know why? The reason you notice no difference is that there isn't any. All the time while you're breathing out, there's air forcing its way in. It's trying to push past. Breathe in again. [*He reflects for a moment.*] Do you ever feel as though the air you're getting is the wrong kind of air?

SECOND COMEDIAN: I just don't get the air, Doctor.

FIRST COMEDIAN: Somebody must have it if you don't.

SECOND COMEDIAN: It's my lungs, Doctor.

FIRST COMEDIAN: Nonsense. There's nothing wrong with your lungs. They're both perfectly fit.

SECOND COMEDIAN: I don't think they hit it off, Doctor. They're at daggers drawn practically the whole time. Over the air.

FIRST COMEDIAN: And your breathing's twisted to blazes as a result. Let me see your tongue. Open your mouth. [*He looks inside.*] You've had this jaw to pieces, haven't you?

SECOND COMEDIAN: It was some years ago, Doctor.

FIRST COMEDIAN: It doesn't matter how long ago it was. It's not a question of time. You laymen start dismantling these parts, but you've no idea how to put them together again. Here's a tooth which has been put back upside down. You're biting on the root.

[FIRST COMEDIAN *begins to use the stethoscope.*]

SECOND COMEDIAN: I've been told I can expect all my teeth to turn turtle eventually.

FIRST COMEDIAN: What are you doing about it?

SECOND COMEDIAN: Consulting you, Doctor.

FIRST COMEDIAN: I thought you'd come to me about your feet.

[FIRST COMEDIAN *grimaces as he continues to sound* SECOND COMEDIAN's *chest.*]

FIRST COMEDIAN: What on earth are you carrying round in the blood stream of yours?

SECOND COMEDIAN: Only my blood, Doctor.

FIRST COMEDIAN: You've got a hell of a noisy circulation.

SECOND COMEDIAN: I have, Doctor. It keeps me awake.

FIRST COMEDIAN: I should think so. It sounds like a mobile iron foundry. You need a silencer for it. I'll give you a letter to take to the King's Cross Blood, Brain, and Bowel Hospital. You can have it under the National Health.

SECOND COMEDIAN: I'd like them to look at my arteries while I'm there as well, Doctor. They seem to have venous blood in them.

FIRST COMEDIAN: It's when you get arterial blood in the veins that you need to begin worrying. Turn over and let me look at your back.

[SECOND COMEDIAN *turns painfully over and* FIRST COMEDIAN *stands looking for some moments in silence.*]

SECOND COMEDIAN: I've had it some time, Doctor.

FIRST COMEDIAN: I can see that. And we can write off these kidneys.

SECOND COMEDIAN: I hardly ever use them, Doctor.

FIRST COMEDIAN: How long have your ribs been like this?

SECOND COMEDIAN: As long as I can remember, Doctor.

FIRST COMEDIAN: And how long is that? Months? Years?

SECOND COMEDIAN: I can't altogether recall, Doctor.

[FIRST COMEDIAN *goes back to his desk where he takes up a pen and begins writing briskly.*]

FIRST COMEDIAN: You can get your clothes on.

[*While* SECOND COMEDIAN *gets dressed,* FIRST COMEDIAN *goes on writing. When* SECOND COMEDIAN *reappears, he puts down his pen.*]

FIRST COMEDIAN: Sit down, Mr Avalanche.

[SECOND COMEDIAN *sits down hesitantly and waits for* FIRST COMEDIAN *to begin.*]

FIRST COMEDIAN: I don't suppose there's much I can tell you that you don't know already. It's an obsolete body, of course, as you realize. And I'm afraid you'll have to do the best you can with it. You must learn to cooperate with your organs.

ECOND COMEDIAN: The small of my back is too big, Doctor.

IRST COMEDIAN: There's nothing to be gained by pretending it isn't. In fact I'll be quite frank with you, Mr Avalanche — it's a great deal larger than it should be. Not only in your case, but with a surprisingly large number of people. But there's absolutely no need for you to have any misgivings about it. People go on — some of them with far less wrong with them than you have by a long way — they go on living active lives sometimes for years. There's no reason at all, Mr Avalanche, why given time you shouldn't have a good twenty or thirty years in front of you.

ECOND COMEDIAN: With a transparent pelvis, Doctor?

IRST COMEDIAN: The main thing is to keep that blood circulating. Take precautions, but don't overdo it. Sleep whenever you can with your eyes closed. Keep off strong poisons of all kinds — and breathe. Breathe all the time. If it doesn't seem to be showing results, make sure it isn't because you're under water. Keep at it: the more you breathe the better you'll feel.

ECOND COMEDIAN: I've been having a lot of trouble with my slanting bowel since I became allergic to smells, Doctor.

IRST COMEDIAN: You will for a time, but it's nothing to worry about. Take this letter to the Blood, Brain, and Bowel Hospital and they'll give you a thorough overhaul.

ECOND COMEDIAN: I shall feel a lot easier, Doctor.

IRST COMEDIAN: And get those feet seen to. They'll be no good to you while they swivel. You should be seeing somebody about them. The feet should never swivel. Hand that letter in to the almoner and you can come back here when the specialist has seen you.

ECOND COMEDIAN: Thank you, Doctor. And I'll come in again as you say when I've been examined.

IRST COMEDIAN: Next Thursday. I can't see you before then. And I'll give you something for those elbows to see if we can't get them bending the right way.

ECOND COMEDIAN: Very good, Doctor.

[SECOND COMEDIAN *goes listlessly out, switching off the light*
he does so. As he enters the living room he switches that light o
BRO *and* MIDDIE PARADOCK *withdraw from the hatch and clo*
it. MIDDIE PARADOCK *half opens the door into the passage throug*
which the Second Comedian has gone.]

MRS PARADOCK: You can find your own way upstairs I expec
You'll find plenty of hot water up there.

[*She closes the door.*]

MR PARADOCK: It's Aunt Chloe's birthday next week.

MRS PARADOCK: So you keep saying.

MR PARADOCK: We shall have to think of something.

MRS PARADOCK: Unless we send Doris round when she com
home from school?

MR PARADOCK: There's never anything she wants. If you think c
anything, she's always got it. Everything you think of she's go
already.

MRS PARADOCK: Listen. Hear them? Hear them washing thei
make-up off upstairs?

MR PARADOCK: What's the good of sending Doris round?

MRS PARADOCK: Not if she were to burst a paper bag in Aun
Chloe's ear? We could get her a deaf-aid.

MR PARADOCK: I don't see why we should go to all that trouble. I
isn't as if it's her twenty-first.

MRS PARADOCK: I thought that was rather novel when he said
You've had this jaw to pieces.

MR PARADOCK: I was expecting him to make some remark abou
dry rot in the roof of his mouth.

MRS PARADOCK: It was very unpredictable.

MR PARADOCK: Except at the end. That bit about the elbow
bending the wrong way. I could see that coming.

MRS PARADOCK: That wasn't till right at the end.

MR PARADOCK: I could see it coming.

MRS PARADOCK: You mean you think you could see it coming
You're being wise after the event again. If you could see it comin
why didn't you say so before it came? That would have been th
time to say it instead of waiting till it was all over.

MR PARADOCK: Because if I'd said so before it came it would have spoiled it for you.

MRS PARADOCK: How did you know I hadn't seen it coming myself?

MR PARADOCK: Because you'd have said so.

MRS PARADOCK: And spoiled it for you?

MR PARADOCK: You wouldn't have spoiled it for me because I saw it coming all along as you well knew.

MRS PARADOCK: One of these days you'll be wise after the event once too often. Did we give them supper last time?

MR PARADOCK: We've never had them before.

MRS PARADOCK: We would never have had them this time if it had been left to you. You'd better ask them what they want to drink when they come down.

[BRO PARADOCK *goes to the table behind the door where he is unseen at first by the two* COMEDIANS, *who enter, wearing dark lounge suits, as* MIDDIE PARADOCK *goes out.*]

MRS PARADOCK: Here they are. There'll be something ready for you in a few minutes if you'll excuse me while I get it served up.

[*She closes the door behind her.*]

FIRST COMEDIAN: I thought they were going to send us off without anything.

[*They catch sight of Bro Paradock. A difficult pause.*]

MR PARADOCK: You'd like a drink, I expect. I'll get you some clean glasses.

[SECOND COMEDIAN *opens the door and closes it behind* BRO PARADOCK *who goes out with the tray.* FIRST COMEDIAN *shrugs, picks up a magazine, and sits with his back to the audience.*]

SECOND COMEDIAN: You're being a bit casual, aren't you? What about all these people?

FIRST COMEDIAN: Well?

SECOND COMEDIAN: We can't sit down and read magazines.

FIRST COMEDIAN: It's not my job to spoon-feed them.

SECOND COMEDIAN: They'll get restive.

FIRST COMEDIAN: Let them talk among themselves for a time.

[SECOND COMEDIAN *sits doubtfully down with a magazine, but is*

E

increasingly ill at ease. He gives up the effort to read, and standing up, looks across to the First Comedian. Convulsively he turns and makes an agonized attempt to address the audience direct.]

SECOND COMEDIAN [*inarticulate for a few moments*]: Good people . . . [*He can get no further and turns angrily on First Comedian, who is now watching him with interest.*]

SECOND COMEDIAN: Don't just sit there!

FIRST COMEDIAN [*putting down his magazine*]: Now listen to me, Bug. Just take it easy, will you? Sit down and take that look off your face. Give it to a rabbit to wear when it meets a stoat. You look like death.

[SECOND COMEDIAN *sits miserably down.*]

SECOND COMEDIAN: Maybe it isn't your job to spoon-feed them. But it's not mine either.

FIRST COMEDIAN: Then we can both stop worrying. If they don't want to amuse themselves they can make do with silence.

SECOND COMEDIAN: They'll never stand for it.

FIRST COMEDIAN: We can break it up with dialogue from time to time if it would make you any easier. And silence isn't so easy to come by as all that, either, if it comes to that.

SECOND COMEDIAN: It's not what you go to a theatre for. You go to other places for silence. Not a theatre. They'll feel cheated.

FIRST COMEDIAN: It's possible. I've known people feel cheated about some odd things. I've known people buy a bath sponge and do calculations to show that two-thirds of the sponge is made up of holes. And it galls them to think that two-thirds of what they've paid good money for isn't really there. Of course they feel cheated. They have every right to feel cheated. They've been overcharged. They've been overcharged two hundred per cent.

SECOND COMEDIAN: Not with a sponge. They've no right to feel cheated over a sponge. A sponge is where you expect to find holes. But a theatre is not where you expect to find silence. That's the difference. The holes are there for a purpose in a sponge. They're there to soak up the water.

FIRST COMEDIAN: Now you're bringing a new element into it. Start talking about purpose and you'll have the whole argument bedevilled. Before we know where we are we shall be splitting hairs. No. Leave purpose out of it. They're not there *to* soak up the water. The holes in a sponge soak up the water. It's not the same.

SECOND COMEDIAN: Which is what I said in the first place. The holes are there for a purpose.

FIRST COMEDIAN: Purpose purpose purpose! It isn't purpose – it's coincidence! They happen to be there and they happen to soak up the water. The holes were there long before you or anybody else ever used a sponge in a bath. And that goes for everything else. It goes for sponges and it goes for ... for everything else. What, for instance, is the purpose of the sea? Is it so that sponges can have somewhere to grow? To give fish somewhere to use their gills? Perhaps you want to tell me that oceans exist to cater for submarines? Rather than waste all those submarines on dry land, God in His all-seeing wisdom made the sea. That's how you're arguing. You're arguing from effect back to cause and it's disastrous.

SECOND COMEDIAN: You're going too fast for me. Your mind doesn't work the way mine does. Let me come to it in my own way.

FIRST COMEDIAN: Good God, we're going to be at it all night. Surely you can see the analogy with a sponge. We don't have to run a bath for you and let you get into it, do we? With your ducks and your boats, before you can see a simple analogy?

SECOND COMEDIAN: Offensive swine!

FIRST COMEDIAN: All I'm trying to say is that anyone who starts with the idea of sponge, and starts squeezing water over himself out of it before he lets his mind wander slowly back through the millennia to the beginnings of things, is going the wrong way about it. He'll end up in a paroxysm of wonder. He'll want to start worshipping something, on the spot, while he's still dripping with water and his glasses are steamed up. And for no better reason, for no more compelling reason, than that the entire evolutionary processes of the cosmos seem to him to have been geared for several million years to the task of providing him with something to wash himself with. How marvellous are Thy ways, O Lord! The seasons always working out just right for the crops;

the flowers never forgetting what colour they have to be to attract the right kind of insect and repel the wrong kind, blessed be God! Isn't it wonderful the way it all works out? And if it had worked out quite differently that would have been pretty wonderful too.

SECOND COMEDIAN: What none of this alters, or even begins to make any impression on as far as I can see, is the irrefutable fact that five minutes of dead silence, or even two or three minutes of it, is going to open the flood-gates of their indignation like the bottom coming out of a bag of cement. They won't stomach it.

FIRST COMEDIAN: At the end of three or four minutes of silence, if it would put your mind at rest, we could have a hunting horn.

SECOND COMEDIAN: Where would that get any of us?

FIRST COMEDIAN: Or a horse whinnying. To break the tension. Kettle-drums. Anything like that.

SECOND COMEDIAN: Bringing a neighing horse on to the stage is going to present us with more problems than it solves.

FIRST COMEDIAN: A whinnying horse. I said nothing about a neighing horse.

SECOND COMEDIAN: People won't stand for it.

FIRST COMEDIAN: As for problems, of course a horse on the stage presents problems. Of course it does. And suppose we solve all the problems it presents? What happens? We end up with more problems than we started with. Because that's the way problems propagate their species. A problem left to itself dries up or goes rotten. But fertilize a problem with a solution – you'll hatch out dozens. It's better than breeding budgerigars. There isn't anything very challenging about a budgerigar. There's a limit to what you can do by way of experiment. Horse-breeding and dog-breeding and all the other hobbies people have to occupy them when they're not breeding problems are not for you and me. The people who count are the ones who devote their lives to a search for the sterile solutions from which no further problems can be bred. I hope they never find it. The moment they do the world ends.

SECOND COMEDIAN: Don't let my presence on the stage cramp your style. Go on as if I weren't here. Make a full-blooded soliloquy of it while you're in voice. Open the hatches and disgorge. Give us all plenty to flounder in and damned be him that first cries, 'Hold, enough!' Only count me out.

[*As* SECOND COMEDIAN *makes to fling open the door,* MIDDIE PARADOCK *enters, carrying a tray of food.*]

MRS PARADOCK: Oh. [*She pauses uncertainly, and then goes to the table to put down the tray.*] I hope I haven't interrupted you both in the middle of a quarrel.

[BRO PARADOCK *enters with a tray of drinks which he puts down on the small table behind the door.*]

MR PARADOCK: You'd like an aperient I expect.

MRS PARADOCK: Put it down and leave it. They can pour their own in a moment.

MR PARADOCK: Oh.

[MIDDIE PARADOCK *takes* BRO PARADOCK *aside.*]

MRS PARADOCK: We've come in at the wrong moment. They were about to have a set to.

[*They go towards the door.*]

MR PARADOCK: Is there anything you need? Or can you manage?

MRS PARADOCK: Of course they don't need anything. There are knives in the drawer if they want to go at each other in that way.

[BRO *and* MIDDIE PARADOCK *go out and close the door.* SECOND COMEDIAN *goes to the small table where he pours out two glasses of the purple drink and brings them to the larger table on which* FIRST COMEDIAN *has set out the food.*
They sit and begin their meal, eating and drinking for some time in silence.]

SECOND COMEDIAN [*holding up his glass*]: This is like the milk of paradise.

[*They continue to eat in silence.*]

SECOND COMEDIAN: It'll save time if we test for humour now.

FIRST COMEDIAN: Afterwards.

SECOND COMEDIAN: Where I get baffled is over isolating the quintessential comic element.

[*Pause.*]

SECOND COMEDIAN: You could get rid of the linguistic overtones by using Esperanto, but that means evening classes for comedian and audience alike while they're all learning Esperanto.

FIRST COMEDIAN: They might not like the joke any more in Esperanto than they did in English.

SECOND COMEDIAN: And after months of part-time study they'll be in a pretty ugly mood.

FIRST COMEDIAN: It's the wrong approach altogether. If you want to isolate the quintessential comic element, the only way you can do it is through your laughter response index.

SECOND COMEDIAN: You mean through my own, personal laughter response index? Because if so there's nothing doing there. Every joke I've ever thought of has been tried out on myself first.

FIRST COMEDIAN: And what's your laughter response index?

SECOND COMEDIAN: I get a nil reading. I've got no sense of humour.

FIRST COMEDIAN: I doubt that. You may have a low laughter quotient. Many people have. But it's ridiculous for a comedian to be without a sense of humour altogether.

SECOND COMEDIAN: I keep it under control. I like to keep my satiric vision unimpaired.

FIRST COMEDIAN: Satiric vision my sun-glasses! You've got about as much satiric vision as a hawk with bi-focals has got eyes like a lynx. Or vice versa as far as that goes. You remind me of a lark walking the plank with its eyes closed. Slowly. Cautiously. Feeling its way step by step, making a false move and clutching convulsively at the air before hitting the water.

[*They continue the meal in silence.*]

FIRST COMEDIAN: You remind me of a pigeon coming down by parachute.

[*Silence.*]

FIRST COMEDIAN: Coming down by parachute because it likes to keep its neuroses airborne as long as possible.

SECOND COMEDIAN: You're as smug as a parrot.

FIRST COMEDIAN: You remind me of a cormorant.

SECOND COMEDIAN: As smug as a parrot from the Azores. I only hope when you hit the water you don't find it frozen over. O that if you do you're wearing your skates. If you're wearing your skates when you hit the water and find it frozen over, you can be as smug as you like till kingdom come and I wish you joy of it. Till then leave it to the parrots, please.

IRST COMEDIAN: You remind me of a cormorant with a beak a yard long tapping out a manifesto to the cosmos on a second-hand typewriter. I affirm letter by tipsy letter that I exist! I am in revolt (with reservations) against revolt! I do not choose not to be! Beak first it plunges like a kingfisher into the glutinous mud, sticks fast and quivers like a tuning-fork.

[*They eat the rest of their meal in silence, and then pushing back their chairs get up from the table.*]

IRST COMEDIAN: I wonder what kind of an allegory they'll make of that.

ECOND COMEDIAN: We shall know soon enough.

[*They move in an unsettled way about the room, picking up and putting down books and ornaments, looking out of the window, yawning.*]

IRST COMEDIAN: I suggest we have one more drink and then see what we can do on the strength of it by way of getting the curtain down.

[*He pours two drinks, one of which he hands to* SECOND COMEDIAN.]

IRST COMEDIAN: Go for spontaneity. Just give the dialogue its head – it's bound to be almost played out by now.

ECOND COMEDIAN: This seems a damned hit or miss way to me of doing things.

IRST COMEDIAN: It won't when you've had some more nectar. Drink up. A sort of rallentando close should do it very nicely but don't try to force it. Let it take its course.

[FIRST COMEDIAN *takes up a position at the window.*]

IRST COMEDIAN: The stars are a long way off tonight.

[SECOND COMEDIAN *joins him for a moment at the window, looks up as though to verify First Comedian's observation, and then turns away.*]

ECOND COMEDIAN: The planets are not much nearer.

[SECOND COMEDIAN *stands looking intently at a goldfish in a bowl.*

FIRST COMEDIAN *comes away from the window.*]

FIRST COMEDIAN: In 1751 Dr Joseph Priestley was distressed that he could not feel a proper repentance for the sin of Adam.

[SECOND COMEDIAN *continues to stare into the goldfish bowl.* FIRST COMEDIAN *has something on his mind which he is uncertain how best to put into words. He takes up a position behind a high-backed chair as though in front of a rostrum.*]

SECOND COMEDIAN: The open sea is a closed book to this goldfish. [*Pause.* SECOND COMEDIAN *turns away from the goldfish.*]

FIRST COMEDIAN: I concede that the earth could be flat. But I doubt it. I doubt it for a number of reasons which I don't intend to go into now. I'd like to put it to the test. I'd very much like to put the whole theory to the test simply by sailing west as far as I could go. If my reckoning is reliable, and if the earth is, as I believe, spherical, I ought eventually, unless there happens to be other land in the way, to arrive on the coast of China.

SECOND COMEDIAN: It's a persuasive theory.

FIRST COMEDIAN: It opens up so many possibilities. Take the sun. We talk about sunrise and sunset. How do we know that what we imagine to be the sun rising and the sun setting, and what we imagine to be the sun moving from east to west across the sky, aren't all in fact a simple optical illusion? How do we know that it isn't we who are moving, while the sun remains motionless in the heavens?

SECOND COMEDIAN: I suppose anything could be an optical illusion.

FIRST COMEDIAN: Look at it this way. This is very tentative, but you've been in a train often enough, haven't you, when another train is drawn up alongside it. Now. One train begins to move. You can feel nothing, but you look through the window and decide that it's the other train which is moving backwards. As you gather speed, however, the movement of your own train as it begins to sway tells you that in fact it is you who are moving forwards.

SECOND COMEDIAN: I think some of this has been gone into before

FIRST COMEDIAN: You'd get exactly the same effect as you go

with the trains if the earth were to be spinning in the opposite direction to the apparent movement of the sun across the sky.

SECOND COMEDIAN: In fact there are a good many people who seem to organize their lives on some such assumption.

FIRST COMEDIAN: I don't intend to let this rest here. If Columbus was right on this score, he was very likely right on other things too. But no one will ever know what those things were until someone takes the trouble to find out. And people aren't going to go to the trouble of finding out until he's been proved right on this point first. That's why it's up to me to vindicate him if I can. I'm certain he was right.

SECOND COMEDIAN: He bides his time who's stuck knee-deep in lime.

FIRST COMEDIAN: I can't see what that's got to do with it.

SECOND COMEDIAN: It's a proverb.

FIRST COMEDIAN: You seem to set precious little store by relevance, I must say.

SECOND COMEDIAN: I prefer to go off at a tangent.

FIRST COMEDIAN: And damned smug you sound about it, too!

SECOND COMEDIAN: I stand for the line of least resistance.

FIRST COMEDIAN: Then let's both doze off.

[*They sit opposite each other and close their eyes. Both begin muttering under their breath. At last* FIRST COMEDIAN *opens his eyes suspiciously. Suspicion turns to anger, and leaping up he gestures violently to where* SECOND COMEDIAN *is sitting bolt upright and with eyes now open.*]

FIRST COMEDIAN: You cavalier bastard! You've been talking in my sleep!

SECOND COMEDIAN: How was I to know whose sleep it was?

FIRST COMEDIAN: You could have asked, couldn't you?

SECOND COMEDIAN: What the hell!

FIRST COMEDIAN: It was a pretty cavalier thing to do, that's all I'm saying. You might ask next time.

[*Both subside. There is a pause.* SECOND COMEDIAN *gets up from his chair.*]

SECOND COMEDIAN: Not a year passes but I am older.

[*Pause.*]

FIRST COMEDIAN: By how much I grow older, by so much am I nearer my end.

[*Pause.*]

SECOND COMEDIAN: When the end comes there is no more.

[*Both look up at the curtain, which begins to fall very slowly. They follow it down a short way with their eyes, turn to look at each other in mutual search for confirmation, find it, and rush to pour themselves another drink. They drink to success as the* CURTAIN *comes quickly down.*]

SCENE 2

Later the same evening.

> [*In front of the curtain appears a man of perhaps thirty-five, well dressed and easy mannered; he would pass for a third-generation estate agent with an office in Knightsbridge. He represents the author. He has a glass in his hand, which is half full of a bright, purple liquid.*]

AUTHOR: I agree. A pretty epileptic start. We're going to see what we can do in the next scene about pulling the thing together. Because this isn't at all, of course, how I wrote the play. You must have realized that. We're all – what shall I say? – we're all just a thought oiled over on this side of the footlights. I expect you've gathered that. And, of course, the thing was by no means as straight-forward as I could have wished even before this crate arrived back-stage. It really is remarkable stuff, I might say. Milk of paradise is . . . well, it's not what I would have called it but I can see the connexion; anyone casting around for some phrase to just hit it off with might well seize on one like that. And of course one is quite possibly not as clear-headed after two or three glasses of this as to be able to explain altogether clearly what it is one is trying to do. Conversely, as it were, such an explanation would hardly have been needed had one not failed – rather lamentably, I must admit – to achieve what one was trying to achieve. How close we're getting to the original tonight is anybody's guess – it would have been anybody's guess whether this nectar had arrived so unexpectedly or not. Because I know hardly a word of Portuguese, and of course Portuguese is precisely the language, unfortunately, in which the play – or most of it – came to me. I was pretty much in the dark, I can tell you, until I got to work with a dictionary. I had someone help me, naturally, and between us we've hammered out something, but I'm far from happy about the whole thing. I think what you'd all better do is to visualize if you can a regimental sergeant-major on a kitchen chair in the middle of a bare stage with his back to you. He has a megaphone through which quite suddenly he'll begin reciting

'Jabberwocky' over and over again for three hours at top speed. I want that image to be clear in your minds, and I want you to hold it there throughout this performance of ours tonight. It is our sheet anchor. Without that image in our minds we shall lose all sense of proportion about what we're going through here and now. For let us make no mistake about it, we are in this together and we must do what we can to see that no one of us suffers more than another. There is no desire, no intention on my part, or on the part of any of us on this side of the footlights, to impose upon you any ready-made idea of our own as to what this play ought to turn out to be. So often the author – we have all known him – moves invisibly among his audience nudging one and distracting another, muttering and mouthing among his betters. Or he leans forward from time to time to make simultaneous overtures of sumptuous impropriety to every Aunt Edna in the house. Such has never been my conception of the relationship that should exist between us. No. It is together that we must shape the experience which is the play we shall all of us have shared. The actors are as much the audience as the audience themselves, in precisely the same way that the audience are as much the actors as the actors themselves. We are all spectators of one another, mutual witnesses of each other's discomfiture. Each of us as he receives his private trouncings at the hands of fate is kept in good heart by the moth in his brother's parachute, and the scorpion in his neighbour's underwear. So let us in the name of that *Schadenfreude* that binds us each to each work from now on together, you on your side of the footlights, and we on ours. We shall need all you can give us. Dramatic situations, plot, glamour, spectacle, lyricism. And some tragic relief. And if we could possibly step up the intellectual content at all? Some of you these days are travelling in from places as far out as Harrow and Morden, and you just have to have your minds stimulated more than in the days when the illusion of thought had to last no farther than Hammersmith or Putney. So there it is. I'll go off now into the wings. We'll leave the stage quite empty for a moment or two, and I think that if like Quakers we all compose our minds in a kind of mystic amalgam, something may come of it.

[*He goes off as the curtain rises on the living room as it was at the end of the first scene. The two* COMEDIANS *are sprawled, fast asleep, in armchairs.* BRO *and* MIDDIE PARADOCK *have just come in.*]

MRS PARADOCK: I'm not saying it's your fault.

MR PARADOCK: Not a drain.

MRS PARADOCK: I'm not saying it's your fault. All I'm saying is that to give them two bottles, both practically full, is hardly the best way to go about things if you want to conserve your nectar.

MR PARADOCK: They might have shown a bit more restraint than to swallow the lot. They call themselves comedians. I'd like to know what's supposed to be comic about drinking to excess.

MRS PARADOCK: They haven't got to be comic the whole time.

MR PARADOCK: I wouldn't employ them to sell typewriter ribbons.

MRS PARADOCK: Neither would anybody else while they were in that state.

MR PARADOCK: It doesn't take you long to leap to their defence, I notice. I wonder if you'd find it so comic if I started drinking to excess.

MRS PARADOCK: You've never done anything to excess in your life. That's just your trouble.

MR PARADOCK: I happen to prefer moderation.

MRS PARADOCK: You make a vice of it. You've never known when not to stop.

MR PARADOCK: I wouldn't employ them to sell typewriter ribbons for me.

MRS PARADOCK: So you keep saying.

MR PARADOCK: No more would I.

MRS PARADOCK: And while you're not employing them selling typewriter ribbons other people are stealing a march on you in some other trade.

MR PARADOCK: Comedians! I'd like to know what's comic about them now. Look at them. It isn't as if they're lying where anyone could trip over them and fall flat on his face. That might raise a laugh if it were someone else; but who's going to fall over them there?

MRS PARADOCK: They'll come round presently.

MR PARADOCK: All I can say is that I hope you're right.

MRS PARADOCK: I wish that were all you could say. Except that you'd go on saying it all day long like a mentally deficient parakeet.

MR PARADOCK: A parakeet wouldn't necessarily have to be mentally deficient to keep saying the same thing over and over again. If that's all it's been taught, how can it say anything else? There's nothing mentally deficient about a parakeet acting according to its nature. It may be educationally subnormal, but that's another matter.

MRS PARADOCK: And when these two come round, which is more to the point, they're going to want some help in making us laugh. You'd better get down Bergson.

MR PARADOCK: They may hit us over the head with it when they come round. [*He goes to the bookshelf.*]

MRS PARADOCK: It isn't very heavy. It's only a small book. I can see it from here – on the shelf. Not that one – that's right – now to the left next to the blue one.

MR PARADOCK [*taking down the book*]: *Laughter.* Henri Bergson.

MRS PARADOCK: It's not big enough to do any damage even if they do hit you over the head with it. Now turn to page thirty-two and read out what it says.

MR PARADOCK [*reads*]: The fundamental law of life . . . [*Gestures to the audience.*] Will they want to take notes?

MRS PARADOCK: They can read it for themselves when they get home.

MR PARADOCK: Oh. [*Reads*] The fundamental law of life . . . is a complete negation of repetition! But I find that a certain movement of head or arm, a movement always the same, seems to return at regular intervals. If I notice it and it succeeds in diverting my attention, if I wait for it to occur and it occurs when I expect it, then involuntarily I laugh. Why? Because I now have before me a machine that works automatically. This is no longer life, it is automatism established in life and imitating it. It belongs to the comic.

MRS PARADOCK: Good. And what does he say on page fifty-eight?

MR PARADOCK: He says. We laugh every time a person gives us the impression of being a thing. You've marked it, but where does all this get us?

MRS PARADOCK: You'll see. These two are Bergson trained.

MR PARADOCK: They'll be like that for hours yet.

[*The two* COMEDIANS *begin to stir.*]

MRS PARADOCK: Will they?

[*The two* COMEDIANS *look around as though coming out of a trance.* SECOND COMEDIAN *leaves his chair and advances to the front of the stage.* FIRST COMEDIAN *follows.*]

SECOND COMEDIAN: You could call this intellectual slapstick.

FIRST COMEDIAN: We are, metaphysically, the Marx Brothers.

SECOND COMEDIAN: Presenting the custard pie comedy of the abstract.

FIRST COMEDIAN: Quintessentially.

SECOND COMEDIAN: And working to a blueprint.

FIRST COMEDIAN: The fundamental law of life is a complete negation of repetition! But I find that a certain movement of head or arm, a movement always the same, seems to return at regular intervals. [BRO PARADOCK *looks, as he begins to recognize these words, with some astonishment towards his wife, who with a complacent half-smile sits down in one of the vacated armchairs and takes up some knitting.*] If I notice it and it succeeds in diverting my attention, if I wait for it to occur and it occurs when I expect it, then involuntarily I laugh. Why? Because I now have before me a machine that works automatically. This is no longer life, it is automatism established in life and imitating it. It belongs to the comic.

SECOND COMEDIAN: We laugh every time a person gives the impression of being a thing.

[BRO PARADOCK *comes forward to join them. The two* COMEDIANS *adopt stage American accents.*]

MR PARADOCK: Tell me something about this Bergson method.

FIRST COMEDIAN: You've never seen Bergson?

MR PARADOCK: Not that I can remember.

FIRST COMEDIAN: He's never seen Bergson.

SECOND COMEDIAN: I thought everybody had seen Bergson sometime or another.

FIRST COMEDIAN: You can't put it into words. You've just got to see it.

MR PARADOCK: I understand he does it all by machinery.

SECOND COMEDIAN: He just comes on. That's all. He comes on like he's a machine.

MRS PARADOCK [*without looking up from her knitting*]: It sounds richly comic.

SECOND COMEDIAN: Remember that time he came on the way he was an electronic computer, and then had them put straw in his hair?

MR PARADOCK: Can he do anything else? Can he do typewriters?

FIRST COMEDIAN: He never has. What about it, Bug? Can Bergson do a typewriter?

MRS PARADOCK: He only wants to start selling you typewriter ribbons. It's a new sideline. Take no notice.

SECOND COMEDIAN: Typewriters don't make out too good comedy-wise, I guess.

MR PARADOCK: I want to be made up to look like an electric computer. I want to raise a laugh.

FIRST COMEDIAN: It's no good looking like an electronic computer. You've got to *be* an electronic computer.

MR PARADOCK: If Bergson can be an electronic computer for the laughs, so can I. What does an electronic computer do?

FIRST COMEDIAN: Electronic computer? It's . . . well, it's electronic. What would you say was the difference, Bug?

SECOND COMEDIAN: What difference?

FIRST COMEDIAN: It's like the human brain except it's electronic.

SECOND COMEDIAN: It's just the way they do things. They do it different. Why can't you stop asking questions?

FIRST COMEDIAN: It thinks. Does calculations. Almost any calculation you like to think of as long as you feed the data into it first.

MR PARADOCK: Why don't we do calculations?

SECOND COMEDIAN: Hell.

MR PARADOCK: For the laughs. Multiply. Subtract. Like an adding machine.

FIRST COMEDIAN: But there are three of us.

MR PARADOCK: A comptometer then. What does it matter? Tell me to do something. Go on. Feed me some data.

FIRST COMEDIAN: What sort of data?

MR PARADOCK: Any sort. Just feed me. Tell me to add a hundred and ninety-three to six hundred and thirty-eight. Any damn thing.

SECOND COMEDIAN: For crying out loud a comptometer's got rows of black keys all over the top of it for crissake with numbers on!

MR PARADOCK: Eight hundred and thirty-one!

SECOND COMEDIAN: They gotta be pressed down.

MR PARADOCK: That's the operator's job. Feed me some data.

FIRST COMEDIAN: And where's your lever mechanism?

MR PARADOCK: Did Bergson say anything about lever mechanism? The cube root of fifty thousand six hundred and fifty-three. . . .

FIRST COMEDIAN [to Second Comedian]: Unless he's electrically operated?

SECOND COMEDIAN: It'd be more kinda realistic to have him bending forward like he was the right shape for a comptometer.

MR PARADOCK: Thirty-seven!

FIRST COMEDIAN: I want him plugged in somewhere.

MR PARADOCK: Three hundred and ninety-six thousand gallons of petrol at three and ninepence three farthings a gallon allowing two per cent wastage . . . .

[FIRST COMEDIAN passes his hands over Bro Paradock in search of something, finds what he wants in his left pocket, and putting his hand into the pocket brings out a three-pin plug attached to a length of flex. This plays itself out from Bro Paradock's pocket.]

SECOND COMEDIAN: Bend him forward.

FIRST COMEDIAN: Like this?

SECOND COMEDIAN: He ought to look more like he's got keys.

MR PARADOCK: Seventy-five thousand five hundred and ninety-four pounds fifteen shillings!

SECOND COMEDIAN: Get him plugged in. For God's sake get him plugged in.

MR PARADOCK: Feed me some data.

FIRST COMEDIAN: Pay that flex out, Bug, will you? I'll plug him in to the power point.

MR PARADOCK: Five times the cube root of pi r squared! Give me a value for r. In centimetres. Furlongs. Cubits. Any damn thing.

[FIRST COMEDIAN *fits plug into socket.*]

SECOND COMEDIAN: Switch it on.

FIRST COMEDIAN: Oh. [*He does so.*] There. Now he's live.

[BRO PARADOCK *twitches and becomes tense. His face begins to work. Suddenly words burst out in a rapid torrent.*]

MR PARADOCK: Paraparaparallelogrammatical. Eighteen men on a dead man's chest at compound interest is not what it's for for four in the morning when the square on the hypotenuse is worth two in the circle two in the circle two in the circle two in the circle . . .

FIRST COMEDIAN [*looks across, alarmed, at Second Comedian*]: He's shorting!

SECOND COMEDIAN: The voltage wants fixing.

[BRO PARADOCK *continues his monologue while* FIRST COMEDIAN *hurries to wrench out the plug.*]

MR PARADOCK: Two in the circle two in the circle two in the circle two in the circle [*plug comes out*] two in the circle [*more calmly and increasingly slowly*] at seven and six, and six and five, and five and four, and four and three, and three and two in the circle at six and five, and five and four, and four and three, and three and two in the circle at five and four, and four and three, and three and two in the circle at four and three, and three and two in the circle at three and two, and one, and nought.

[BRO PARADOCK *unbends and mops his brow.*]

MR PARADOCK: I thought I was never going to get back. Who unplugged me?

SECOND COMEDIAN: You were shorting.

MR PARADOCK: You were pressing the wrong buttons. You can't do all that about pi r squared and compound interest on a comptometer. That's not what it's for. Of course I was shorting.

FIRST COMEDIAN: You went haywire.

MR PARADOCK: I'm not surprised.

MRS PARADOCK [*getting up*]: I expect you'd all like some coffee after that.

SECOND COMEDIAN: Thank you, Mrs Paradock. We would.

MRS PARADOCK: You and Hamster will want it black, I expect, after your drunken orgy.

FIRST COMEDIAN: Yes, please, Mrs Paradock. I think we finished up both those two bottles your husband opened for us.

SECOND COMEDIAN: I feel terrible.

MRS PARADOCK: I shan't be long. You'll feel better for a cup of coffee.

[MIDDIE PARADOCK *goes out.* BRO PARADOCK *and the two* COMEDIANS *dispose themselves about the room as the lights fade out. A spotlight reveals a technician in a white coat on right. The living room remains in darkness while the technician comes forward and addresses the audience.*]

TECHNICIAN: I don't want to hold up the action for more than a minute or two, and in fact I have no intention of holding it up for as long as that. What we are doing here on the technical side is rather new and I have been asked to come out here on the stage and as quickly as I can without holding up the action longer than absolutely necessary to give you in a few words if I can just what it is we are trying to do on the technical side. You are not going to be approached in any way. Please be quite at ease on that score. This is not audience participation in any new and more exasperating form so do please relax and be quite natural. What we are doing is by way of being an experiment and it is an experiment we can only carry through successfully by at some stage in the production taking the audience – that is your good selves – into our confidence. We do this as much for our own sake as yours. We want you to be quite spontaneous. And that is why I am here now. To take you into our confidence. It is as I say a new technique and we do have of course a huge barrier to break down of prejudice if not outright hostility from those who are not fully conversant with what we are trying to do. Any opportunity of making our aims and methods more widely known is something we are always very glad to have extended to us and I on this occasion am very grateful to both you and those responsible for this production for being allowed to put you in the picture. This is a technique which can be used for any kind of stage production. Any production whatever that it is possible to mount on a stage where we have apparatus installed comes within our scope. But it is absolutely essential in every case for the audience to be as it were receptive to the need, if we are to be one hundred per cent effective, of as I say complete spontaneity. What we want, briefly, are your reactions. As you know all of us react in the theatre. Laughter. Laughter is nothing more or less than a reaction. If we instinctively feel something to be funny, we laugh. In other words, we react. Now we have literally thousands of feet of microfilm on which we have recorded these reactions as and when they have occurred. These recordings we match up with recordings made on other reels of microfilm, recordings of whatever on the stage has acted as the stimulus for each reaction recorded. Let me illustrate. At one point in the performance, shall we say, a witticism comes into play. This witticism is picked up by our very sensitive detectors which also break it down into molecules. There is a reason for this. An author who makes use of our records gains a complete and accurate picture not only of the effectiveness of a given witticism as a whole, but is enabled to see, as though under a microscope, just which *part* of that witticism achieved maximum response. So you can see how essential it is that every member of the audience should react at optimum spontaneity from beginning to end of the performance. This ensures that at any given stage in the production the laughter response index which we pass on to the author and producer is as accurate and reliable as science can make it. Because that of course is what we are out to do. We hope in time with the cooperation of theatre managements and audiences all over the country to build up in microfilm a library which will embody the case histories in terms of audience reaction of a sufficiently large and representative number of productions of all kinds to do away with the need for inspired guesswork on the part of author or producer. Will this be funny? Or is one part of this likely to be more funny than some other, perhaps less funny, part? This is the kind of question the writer of comedy is always having to ask himself, and it's the kind of question we on the technical side feel we can supply a reliable answer to. And not only of course the writer of comedy. In tragedy too – where of course the response to be successful must always be a rather different response from that evoked by comedy – I hope I'm not holding up the action too much, but what we do feel we want to get established, and get more and more established, is the very real part we on the technical side can play. As I say, the writer of tragedy with his stock-in-trade of pity and terror is working just as much in the dark as his colleague of the comic muse. How much pity? Just what degree of terror? And so on. If there was audience resistance, what caused it? This is another question which, by classifying the laughter and tears we pick up, we can often answer for the bewildered author. If his audience according to our records are viscerotonic endomorphs this may explain why this play, written shall we say, for cerebrotonic ectomorphs, fails to achieve saturation impact. And now I think I have held up the production long enough. I would only like to say in conclusion that we have the technique, and are only waiting for the green light to go right ahead and take the guesswork out of the inspiration for the ultimate benefit of you, the audience. Thank you for listening to me – and before I do finally finish I would like to say how much we have been helped, very materially helped, by the way everyone responsible for this production down to the author himself has done everything possible to give us all the facilities we have asked for. And of course you, the audience, have given us what is our very life-blood – your spontaneity. Thank you very much.

[*He goes out. Lights come up in the living room.* BRO PARADOCK *and the two* COMEDIANS *are in various parts of the room, silent and blank.* MIDDIE PARADOCK *enters with a tray of coffee cups and a jug of coffee.*]

MRS PARADOCK: Did you think I was never coming?

MR PARADOCK: Ah, coffee.

MRS PARADOCK: Get the books out, Bro, will you?

FIRST COMEDIAN: Don't get them out for me, Mrs Paradock. I never read.

MRS PARADOCK: Perhaps Bug would like a book with his coffee.

SECOND COMEDIAN: I do like a short book with coffee. Thank you, Mrs Paradock.

MRS PARADOCK: Now come on. Here's a place for you, Bug. Help Hamster to a chair, Bro. He's wearing his shoes crooked this week and I know they're hurting him. There are plenty of books at your elbow, Bug, and more in the bookcase if you want them. Hamster: now what are you reading?

FIRST COMEDIAN: Nothing for me, thank you, Mrs Paradock. Just the coffee.

MRS PARADOCK: I can't get used to you not reading with your coffee.

SECOND COMEDIAN: He never has, Mrs Paradock.

MRS PARADOCK: Are we all settled? Come on, Bro. What are you going to have? Fiction, biography? I think I'll help myself to this textbook.

SECOND COMEDIAN: It looks rather nice.

MRS PARADOCK: Yes. Now we can all have a good read with our coffee.

MR PARADOCK: Shall I see what's on the wireless while we're reading?

MRS PARADOCK: That's right, Bro. See what's on. It ought to be the service.

MR PARADOCK [looking at his watch]: It'll be starting.

[BRO PARADOCK tunes in the wireless and all except FIRST COMEDIAN continue reading throughout. The prayers heard from the wireless are intoned in a voice of cultured Anglican fatuity, and the responses said in low-toned earnestness by a small chorus of voices, which is joined by FIRST COMEDIAN in an undertone.]

PRAYER: . . . weep at the elastic as it stretches:

MR PARADOCK: It's started.

RESPONSE: And rejoice that it might have been otherwise.

PRAYER: Let us sing because round things roll:

RESPONSE: And rejoice that it might have been otherwise.

PRAYER: Let us praise God for woodlice, and for buildings sixty-nine feet three inches high:

RESPONSE: For Adam Smith's *Wealth of Nations* published in 1776:

PRAYER: For the fifth key from the left on the lower manual of the organ of the Church of the Ascension in the Piazza Vittorio Emmanuele II in the town of Castelfidardo in Italy:

RESPONSE: And for gnats.

PRAYER: How flat are our trays:

RESPONSE: Our sewers how underground and rat-infested altogether.

PRAYER: As the roots of a tree strike downwards:

RESPONSE: So fire burns.

PRAYER: As a river flows always towards its mouth:

RESPONSE: So is sugar sweet.

PRAYER: Let us laugh therefore and be glad for the Balearic Islands:

RESPONSE: And sing with joy in the presence of dyspepsia.

PRAYER: Let us give praise for those who compile dictionaries in large buildings, for the gallant men and women on our beaches, for all those who in the fullness of time will go out to meet whatever fate awaits them, for the tall, the ham-fisted, the pompous, and for all men everywhere and at all times.

RESPONSE: Amen.

PRAYER: Let us give thanks for air hostesses and such as sit examinations, for the Bessemer process and for canticles, that all who live in France may be called Frenchmen and that nothing may be called useful that has no purpose.

RESPONSE: Amen.

PRAYER: Let us talk and itch and swim and paint:

RESPONSE: Let us talk and itch and swim and paint.

PRAYER: Let us make music, water, love, and rabbit hutches:

RESPONSE: Let us make music, water, love, and rabbit hutches.

PRAYER: Let us be brave and punctual:

RESPONSE: And vituperative and good-looking.

PRAYER: Let us laugh with those we tickle:

RESPONSE: Let us laugh with those we tickle.

PRAYER: Let us weep with those we expose to tear-gas:

RESPONSE: Let us weep with those we expose to tear-gas.

PRAYER: Let us throw back our heads and laugh at reality:

RESPONSE: Which is an illusion caused by mescalin deficiency.

PRAYER: At sanity:

RESPONSE: Which is an illusion caused by alcohol deficiency.

PRAYER: At knowledge which is an illusion caused by certain bio-chemical changes in the human brain structure during the course of human evolution, which had it followed another course would have produced other bio-chemical changes in the human brain structure, by reason of which knowledge as we now experience it would have been beyond the reach of our wildest imaginings; and by reason of which, what is now beyond the reach of our wildest imaginings would have been familiar and commonplace. Let us laugh at these things. Let us laugh at thought:

RESPONSE: Which is a phenomenon like any other.

PRAYER: At illusion:

RESPONSE: Which is an illusion, which is a phenomenon like any other.

PRAYER: Let us love diversity:

RESPONSE: Because there is neither end nor purpose to it.

PRAYER: Let us love simplicity:

RESPONSE: Because there is neither end nor purpose to it.

PRAYER: Let us think, and think we think, because leaves are green and because stones fall and because volcanoes erupt in a world where seas are salt.

RESPONSE: Amen.

[*The introductory bars of 'Sweet Polly Oliver' in an orchestrated version are heard from the wireless.* FIRST COMEDIAN *gets to his feet.*]

FIRST COMEDIAN: I think this is where we stand, isn't it?

[*The* SECOND COMEDIAN, BRO, *and* MIDDIE PARADOCK *have become aware of the music and begin to stand. Rather self-consciously they join in the hymn-like singing of 'Sweet Polly Oliver'. There is a momentary silence when the song ends, and then to neutralize their embarrassment they all try to be excessively normal.*]

MRS PARADOCK: Now. Have we all had enough coffee?

SECOND COMEDIAN: It was splendid coffee, Mrs Paradock. You must show me how you make it.

MR PARADOCK: Middie's coffee is made by a secret process, Bug. Wild horses wouldn't drag it out of her.

FIRST COMEDIAN: In that case we'll be making up ingenious excuses for coming round here every evening for coffee, Mrs Paradock.

MRS PARADOCK: You're both very welcome. Bro and I need some good comedians in the house to prevent us quarrelling all the time.

SECOND COMEDIAN: That's a bargain then, Mrs Paradock. We supply the comedy, you supply the coffee.

FIRST COMEDIAN: And if our comedy's as good as your coffee, Mrs Paradock, we shall all be more than satisfied.

MRS PARADOCK: Well, if no one wants any more coffee I'll clear away the cups.

[MIDDIE PARADOCK *puts the cups and saucers on to the tray and takes this outside.*]

FIRST COMEDIAN: Did you know that a female cod can be the mother of eight million eggs?

MR PARADOCK: No.

FIRST COMEDIAN: Eight million!

SECOND COMEDIAN: It's the apotheosis of irresponsibility.

MR PARADOCK: There'd be no counting them – not if there were eight million of them. Except on the fingers of eight hundred thousand pairs of hands.

SECOND COMEDIAN: Eight hundred thousand people to count the eggs of a single cod! It's ludicrous.

MR PARADOCK: And yet they call a female god a goddess.

FIRST COMEDIAN: There's no accounting for it.

SECOND COMEDIAN: I'm not sure that I want to account for it. It's one of those things my imagination wilts at.

MR PARADOCK: I always thought you had a pretty strong imagination.

FIRST COMEDIAN: He hasn't. Not for that sort of thing. He picked up an imaginary chair yesterday. I thought he was handling it remarkably easily, and when he sat down on it I knew why. It just crumpled up under him.

SECOND COMEDIAN: I should think Bro has got a strong imagination. Let's see you lift an imaginary chair, Bro, by the back legs.

MR PARADOCK: How?

FIRST COMEDIAN: Get hold of it by the two back legs. Keep your arms straight out in front of you and see if you can bring it up to shoulder height. And hold it there.

MR PARADOCK: Where do I get the chair from?

SECOND COMEDIAN: Imagine it.

MR PARADOCK: Shall I?

FIRST COMEDIAN: Go on.

[BRO PARADOCK *squats on his haunches, gets up and removes his jacket, squats again, and adjusts his position before going through the motions of taking a grip on the back legs of a chair. His efforts to stand up with it are successful but strenuous.* FIRST COMEDIAN *picks up a chair which he places in* BRO PARADOCK'S *outstretched hands. He holds this chair without effort.*]

MR PARADOCK: That's extraordinary! I'd never have believed it.

SECOND COMEDIAN: You were letting your imagination run away with you.

MR PARADOCK: I'd never have believed it. The one I imagined I was lifting was twice as heavy as this one.

FIRST COMEDIAN: You've just got a strong imagination. You're like me. I used it to develop my muscles.

SECOND COMEDIAN: Why don't you two have a contest of strength? We'll ask Mrs Paradock for a pair of scales when she comes in. See which of you can hang the heaviest weight on them.

FIRST COMEDIAN: What do you say, Bro?

MR PARADOCK: I'm game if you are. [*He goes to the door, opens it, and puts his head out.*] Middie! Have we still got those scales?

[MIDDIE PARADOCK *is heard off:* 'As far as I know. What do you want them for?']

MR PARADOCK: I'll go and get them now.

[BRO PARADOCK *goes out. Several seconds later* MIDDIE PARADOCK *comes in, followed by* BRO PARADOCK *with the scales.*]

MRS PARADOCK: I hear you're going to have a trial of strength between you.

SECOND COMEDIAN: Not me, Mrs Paradock. It's these two.

MRS PARADOCK: I'm surprised Bro's got a strong imagination – I'd never have said so.

SECOND COMEDIAN: Who's going to hold the scales? Shall I hold them while you two get ready?

MR PARADOCK: Isn't it going to be a bit heavy for you when we both put weights on the end?

FIRST COMEDIAN: Don't worry about Bug. His imagination isn't as strong as yours and mine, Bro. He won't register more than a pound or two.

SECOND COMEDIAN: I shall be all right. Now then. Here it is. As soon as you're both ready.

MR PARADOCK [*looking at* FIRST COMEDIAN]: Shall we start?

FIRST COMEDIAN: Right. Here goes.

[*Both pretend to be lifting massive weights, with which they stagger towards the scales held by* SECOND COMEDIAN. *As they simultaneously hang their weights on opposite arms of the scales,* SECOND COMEDIAN'S *arm dips slightly as he takes the strain. The balance remains horizontal.*]

MRS PARADOCK: Nothing in it. Fancy that.

MR PARADOCK [*panting*]: I don't know what was in it. It weighed like cement.

MRS PARADOCK: Bug seems to be managing it without much difficulty.

FIRST COMEDIAN: Better put it down now, Bug. It's putting too much strain on the scales. You'll have the joint starting.

SECOND COMEDIAN [*lifting each load on to the floor in turn*]: I don't know about cement. It feels like something a whole lot lighter than cement to me.

MRS PARADOCK: You must be stronger in the muscles, Bug.

FIRST COMEDIAN: It's his imagination, Mrs Paradock. It isn't equal to it.

MRS PARADOCK: Is that what it is?

[*Silence.*]

MRS PARADOCK: You forgot to ring up about the elephant, Bro.

MR PARADOCK: I thought you'd seen about it.

MRS PARADOCK: I have now. They're delivering it in the morning.

SECOND COMEDIAN: As for elephants, I must say we've started a fine lot of hares this evening. Don't you think so?

MR PARADOCK: March hares.

FIRST COMEDIAN: We've started them all right. A whole lot of mad March hares streaking hell for leather across the open country.

SECOND COMEDIAN: And not one but will drop in its tracks before these worthy people pick up the scent.

[*All turn to gaze thoughtfully at the audience.*]

MRS PARADOCK: What a shame we can't give them a run for their money with tortoises.

CURTAIN

ACT TWO

Evening next day.

[*The living room.* BRO PARADOCK, *hands in pockets, is staring thoughtfully out through the window.* MIDDIE PARADOCK *turns away from the window.*]

MRS PARADOCK: It'll have to stay out.

[BRO PARADOCK *turns slowly away and crosses the room.*]

MR PARADOCK: What are the measurements?

MRS PARADOCK: You don't need measurements. A thing that size in a pre-fab.

MR PARADOCK: I thought we were living in a bungalow.

MRS PARADOCK: People will think we're trying to go one better than everybody else.

MR PARADOCK: It's only once a year for goodness' sake! You should have kept the measurements.

MRS PARADOCK: I should have gone for it myself instead of ringing. [*Turns to look out of the window*] Look at it. Look at its great ears flapping about. Surely they know by now what size we always have.

MR PARADOCK: Perhaps they've sent us the wrong one.

MRS PARADOCK: It's big enough for a hotel. If you had a hotel or a private school or something you wouldn't need a thing that size.

MR PARADOCK: I suppose not.

MRS PARADOCK: And supposing it goes berserk in the night? I'm not getting up to it.

MR PARADOCK: Why should it go berserk in the night any more than a smaller one?

MRS PARADOCK: We'll have old Mrs Stencil round again if it does – threatening us with the R.S.P.C.A.

MR PARADOCK: You should have been in when they came with it, then you could have queried the measurements.

MRS PARADOCK: I can't think what we're going to call it. We can't call it Mr Trench again.

MR PARADOCK: The only time we've not called it Mr Trench was three years ago when we had to make do with a giraffe.

MRS PARADOCK: And look at the fuss we had before they'd take it in part exchange.

MR PARADOCK: Of course they made a fuss. There was something wrong with it.

MRS PARADOCK [*looking through the window*]: Imagine calling a clumsy great thing that size Mr Trench.

MR PARADOCK: Why not?

MRS PARADOCK: We can't go on year after year calling it Mr Trench.

MR PARADOCK: You talk as if it were the same animal every time.

MRS PARADOCK: You can hear the neighbours, can't you? They'll think we never launch out.

MR PARADOCK: I know what you want to call it.

MRS PARADOCK: It looks all the time as if we were hard up for a name to give the animal.

MR PARADOCK: You want to call it Oedipus Rex, don't you?

MRS PARADOCK: It's better than Mr Trench year after year. At least it sounds as if we knew what was going on in the world.

MR PARADOCK: Oedipus Rex! [*Wags a finger archly through the window*] Ah, ah! Only the *edible* blooms remember, Oedipus.

MRS PARADOCK: If you say it in that tone of voice of course it sounds ridiculous.

MR PARADOCK [*in same tone*]: Oedipus! Oedipus! You're letting that glass take *all* your weight!

MRS PARADOCK: Anything else would sound equally as ridiculous if you said it like that.

MR PARADOCK: It isn't Mr Trench we want a change from.

MRS PARADOCK: The only thing to do is ring up the Zoo. Tell them to come and collect it.

MR PARADOCK: And be without an elephant at all?

MRS PARADOCK: Tell them to come and collect it and the sooner the better. I'd rather not have one.

MR PARADOCK: I beg to differ.

MRS PARADOCK: We did without one the year we had a giraffe instead.

MR PARADOCK: I know we did without one the year we had a giraffe instead. And look at the trouble we had getting it changed. I don't want that all over again.

MRS PARADOCK: It's the R.S.P.C.A. I'm worried about.

MR PARADOCK: They haven't been round yet. In any case you wouldn't get the Zoo at this time. They'll be closed.

MRS PARADOCK: I don't know why they couldn't send us what we asked for in the first place.

MR PARADOCK: Is it any use trying to get hold of Eddie on the phone?

MRS PARADOCK: Yes. Ring Eddie up. Or Nora. Nora'd be sure to know what to do. They used to keep pigeons and things. They had a room full of nothing else but different kinds of birds when they were all living at No. 89, and white mice and things.

MR PARADOCK: It'll have to stay outside tonight.

MRS PARADOCK: I'm not having it in the kitchen if that's what you're leading up to.

MR PARADOCK: If it starts straying all over the place during the night we shall have the R.S.P.C.A. making a lot of difficulties.

MRS PARADOCK: Not if we get it changed first thing. Get on to Nora.

MR PARADOCK: If we're getting it changed first thing in the morning, where's the sense in thinking up a name like Oedipus Rex for it now?

MRS PARADOCK: Because I'm not calling it Mr Trench six years running. You can if you like. I'm not.

MR PARADOCK: I didn't want to call it Mr Trench the year it was a giraffe. That was your idea. It was your idea it would make a pleasant change to be giving the name to a giraffe instead of an elephant. Now you complain about calling it Mr Trench six years running.

MRS PARADOCK: I think we'd be better off without it.

MR PARADOCK: How would we?

MRS PARADOCK: I do really. I think we'd be better off without
   We've done nothing except bicker ever since they came with
   it.

MR PARADOCK: We weren't in when they came with it.

MRS PARADOCK: That's the whole point.

   [*Both relapse into silence.* BRO PARADOCK *takes up a paper.*]

MR PARADOCK [*looks up after an interval from his paper*]: If we're
   going to change the name at all I can't see what you've got against
   Hodge for that matter.

MRS PARADOCK: Hodge is all right for a monkey.

MR PARADOCK: We'll go through some names and see what we can
   agree on. Hodge.

MRS PARADOCK: Hodge for a monkey. Gush for an elephant.

MR PARADOCK: Admiral Benbow.

MRS PARADOCK: Hiram B. Larkspur.

MR PARADOCK: Playboy.

MRS PARADOCK: Killed-with-kindness Corcoran.

MR PARADOCK: New-wine-into-old-bottles Backhouse.

MRS PARADOCK: 'Tis-pity-she's-a-whore Hignett.

MR PARADOCK: Lucifer.

MRS PARADOCK: Stonehenge.

MR PARADOCK: Haunch.

MR PARADOCK: ⎫
MRS PARADOCK: ⎬ Splinter.

MR PARADOCK: Thank God we can agree on something. Now I can
   ring Eddie.

MRS PARADOCK: Why ring up Eddie when you've got Nora who's
   had experience with animals? She could probably suggest something.

MR PARADOCK: So you keep saying. [*Dialling*]

MRS PARADOCK: Well?

MR PARADOCK: Is that Mrs Mortice? . . . Oh. . . . Will you? Thank
   you.

MRS PARADOCK: You've decided to ring Nora then.

MR PARADOCK [*ignores her*]: Hallo. Nora? . . . Yes, thank you, Nora.
   And how are you? . . . Oh? And what's that, Nora? . . . A what?

... Hold on a moment, Nora.... Yes.... Yes.... Hold on, Nora. Wait till I fetch Middie.

MRS PARADOCK: Don't say they've got ours.

MR PARADOCK: It's a snake. She says they ordered a snake and they've got one that's too short.

MRS PARADOCK: Too short for what?

MR PARADOCK: She says they're worried about the R.S.P.C.A.

MRS PARADOCK [takes up phone]: Nora? ... Yes, Bro was telling me. Isn't it maddening? ... Yes.... Yes – they've done exactly the same with us.... No. About ten times too big. I don't know what the vanman was thinking about. A thing that size in a bunga-low.... Not indoors, no. We've got it out at the back.... Yes. I think you're quite justified.... No.... No.... Not till the morn-ing, Nora. Bro thinks they'll be closed now anyway.

MR PARADOCK: Why not ask her if she'd like to have Mr Trench and we'll take the snake off her.

MRS PARADOCK: What? ... No, I was talking to Bro, Nora. I think he's got some suggestion to make. I'll get him to tell you himself. [Puts her hand over mouthpiece] You talk to her. She's on about this snake of theirs.

MR PARADOCK: What about it, Nora? If yours is on the short side it might do us very nicely ... and you're welcome to Mr Trench. ... Yes. We don't need anything.... No trouble at all, Nora.... Yes? Well, that's better still.... I'll come round with it then.... No.... No, I'll remember.... Yes – in about half an hour, then. Good-bye, Nora.

MRS PARADOCK: Thank goodness we rang them up.

MR PARADOCK: Did she say how short this snake was?

MRS PARADOCK: She didn't give any measurements, if that's what you mean.

MR PARADOCK: I thought perhaps you might have thought to ask her what the measurements were.

MRS PARADOCK: Why didn't you ask her for the measurements yourself, as far as that goes?

MR PARADOCK: How was I to know whether you'd asked already?

MRS PARADOCK: You heard me talking to her.

MR PARADOCK: What have you done with my gumboots?

MRS PARADOCK: What do you want gumboots for to go down the road a few doors with an elephant? Where are your other shoes?

MR PARADOCK: These are my other shoes I've got on.

MRS PARADOCK: And I should come straight back with Mr Trench. We don't want Mrs Stencil asking a lot of questions.

MR PARADOCK: I notice you're all for calling it Mr Trench now you know it's a snake.

MRS PARADOCK: What are you going to bring it back in? You can't have it on a lead like a canary.

MR PARADOCK: In any case I thought we'd settled on Hodge for a name.

MRS PARADOCK: Hodge for a jackal. Gush for an anaconda.

MR PARADOCK: Admiral Benbow.

MRS PARADOCK: Hiram B. Larkspur.

MR PARADOCK: Playboy.

MRS PARADOCK: We'll see how short it is first.

MR PARADOCK: The only thing I've ever seen on a lead is a dog. I've never seen a canary on a lead.

MRS PARADOCK: A dog on a lead then.

MR PARADOCK: I hate this job.

MRS PARADOCK: You say that every year.

MR PARADOCK: I've never had to do it before.

MRS PARADOCK: You say it about other things.

MR PARADOCK: If it comes to that, how do you know it *is* an anaconda?

MRS PARADOCK: What else would it be? We shall have the R.S.P.C.A. round while you stand there.

MR PARADOCK: Good God!

    [*He goes out.*]

MRS PARADOCK [*slowly moving her head from side to side*]: Admiral Benbow!

    [BRO PARADOCK *comes back into the room with collar turned up. He turns it down and shakes rain from his jacket.*]

MRS PARADOCK: You're not back already?

MR PARADOCK: I'm not going in this rain.

MRS PARADOCK: It's barely started.

MR PARADOCK: I don't want to get mixed up in a lot of rain. I haven't got a hat for that sort of thing.

MRS PARADOCK: You've got an eye-shield. What's wrong with that?

MR PARADOCK: You gave it away.

MRS PARADOCK: I don't mean that one. I mean the one you wear for tennis.

MR PARADOCK: But that's to keep the sun out of my eyes.

MRS PARADOCK: Can't you wear it back to front?

[*Pause.*]

MR PARADOCK: What a coincidence! Uncle Fred! That's just what Uncle Fred used to do. When he was at sea. He used to wear an eye-shield back to front rather than be put to the expense of a sou'-wester. It deflected the rainwater from his neck and the elastic band passed conveniently across his mouth like a horse's bit.

[*A knock at the door.* MIDDIE PARADOCK *goes to open it.*]

MRS PARADOCK: That would be too ingenious for you, of course.

[NORA *is at the door.*]

MRS PARADOCK: Nora! You're drenched! Come in.

NORA: I thought I'd better come over with this as soon as I saw it was raining. [*Fumbles in her handbag.*] I'm afraid I get terribly wet in these showers. I just haven't got that kind of a hat, I suppose. [*Takes out a pencil box.*] There, I said it was short, didn't I?

MRS PARADOCK: Good gracious. Do I open it?

MR PARADOCK: That's never an anaconda.

MRS PARADOCK: Would Nora have brought it over if it had been? Perhaps I'll leave it in its loosebox. We don't want it eavesdropping. [*She puts the box, without opening it, on the mantelpiece.*]

NORA [*looks into the mirror*]: Goodness! My make-up.

MRS PARADOCK: Let me see. Oh, no. I think she's done very well, Bro, don't you? I admire you for coming out in it at all.

MR PARADOCK: It's a very good attempt, Nora. It takes a pretty good hat to manage a shower like that one. I didn't even try it. Not with my poor old hat.

NORA: I don't know about that, Bro. I wouldn't mind having a hat like yours anyway.

MRS PARADOCK: Hats aren't everything in this world. Far from it.

MR PARADOCK: I know they aren't everything.

NORA: Some people seem to get by quite nicely without them. In fact I've often noticed it's the ones who haven't any hats at all who live the most satisfying lives in the long run.

MR PARADOCK: It isn't so much having the hats as knowing how to make the best use of them.

MRS PARADOCK: We can't all be blessed with hats.

MR PARADOCK: Look at Mrs Blackboy's husband and the showers he's got through in his time with that plastic shopping bag he carries round on his head.

NORA: Or Bella for that matter. Bella's up half the night sometimes weatherproofing that old straw beehive she goes out in whenever she's got rain to cope with.

MRS PARADOCK: And a lot of those who are supposed to have such wonderful hats are going around half the time in other people's. I haven't got much time for them. They got them out of Christmas crackers more likely than not.

MR PARADOCK: I don't like to see the time Bella spends on millinery. That sort of thing's all right if you've got millinery in your make-up. Otherwise leave it alone.

MRS PARADOCK: Bro's not much of a one for millinery.

MR PARADOCK: I don't get the time. I've got other things to do. Nora and I prefer to leave the showers to the ones with the hats, unless we're compelled to tackle them. And then we don't do too badly, eh, Nora?

MRS PARADOCK: Nora's got plenty of hats, as you well know. Take no notice of him, Nora. He's only acting the fool. You shouldn't be so rude to people, Bro. It's lucky Nora knows you.

NORA: Oh, I've never made any pretensions to hats.

MRS PARADOCK: You're too modest, Nora.

MR PARADOCK: I've always known what I could do, and I've always known what I couldn't do. That's one of the reasons why I never became an air hostess.

NORA: Hasn't your Myrtle got a fine little hat on her head? I was noticing it only the other day.

MRS PARADOCK: I don't know where she gets it from then! Although I must say she didn't do too badly in her storm-test last week. I will give Myrtle her due – she doesn't seem to worry much what weather she goes out in.

MR PARADOCK: She gets it from Stan if she gets it from anybody. Or Uncle Fred.

NORA: Do you know what I think? It would never surprise me if Myrtle didn't turn out to be something of a storm-breaker before she's finished. She's got the hats for it.

MRS PARADOCK: You're joking, Nora.

MR PARADOCK: What about Uncle Fred, then? He did very nicely for himself with his eye-shield.

MRS PARADOCK: Exactly. It's Uncle Fred's eye-shield that got him where he was – you couldn't call him a natural storm-breaker. [*To Nora*] Uncle Fred was Bro's uncle in the navy, Nora.

MR PARADOCK: He used to wear his eye-shield back to front so as to protect his neck from the rainwater.

MRS PARADOCK: Anybody would think he was a positive sou'-wester man the way you talk.

MR PARADOCK: It wasn't that he didn't have a sou'wester, so much as that he could never get round to putting it on.

MRS PARADOCK: He never had one. You know perfectly well he used to borrow quite shamelessly from the other men whenever there was an important storm at sea and he couldn't get by with just his eye-shield.

NORA [*loudly*]: Aha! Whose is the waste-paper basket! It looks rather interesting.

MRS PARADOCK: That's Mr Malden's. We lent him a couple of lampshades Myrtle has grown out of for his little boy; he said we were welcome to his waste-paper basket if we could make anything of it.

MR PARADOCK: It might be all right for Myrtle when she's older. It looks to me like one he had when he was at school.

NORA: I rather think Myrtle's father has got his eye on it, too, i
I'm not too much mistaken.

MRS PARADOCK: He's tried it on for size. Didn't you, Bro? On
night last week. But he won't be seen out in it.

MR PARADOCK: That sort of thing's all right for the summer.

NORA [*looks through the window*]: Thank goodness it seems to hav
stopped raining for the time being anyway.

MRS PARADOCK: Oh splendid. Now you can take Mr Trench acros
to Nora's, Bro.

NORA: I'll have to be going, then. I don't want to be out when yo
call, Bro.

MRS PARADOCK: That would never do, would it?

MR PARADOCK: It was lucky you got here when you did, Nora.
was just setting out. We might have missed each other.

NORA: We might.

MRS PARADOCK: Not if you were both going the same way.

MR PARADOCK: We could hardly be going the same way whe
Nora was going in one direction and I was going in the other. Hov
could we have been going the same way?

MRS PARADOCK: If you like, Nora, I'll hold Bro back for a fev
minutes. That'll give you time to get in and turn round before h
comes knocking on the door. [*She holds him by the collar.*]

NORA: If you're sure it won't throw you out?

MRS PARADOCK: Of course it won't. It's no trouble keeping Br
back for twenty minutes or so. Especially when you're helping u
out by taking the elephant off our hands.

NORA: It'll be nice to get something with some size to it, believ
me. I only hope you find you can make do with Bees' Weddin
there. It was hopelessly short for us.

MRS PARADOCK: You've got the upstairs as well, of course, haven
you?

NORA: And the cellar. We just can't do with anything smaller. We'v
managed in the past with a rhinoceros – we had that one the yea
before last, but it was barely large enough.

MRS PARADOCK: This one's a ridiculous size for us in this bungalow

We always like to have an elephant, of course, if we can, but we can't cope with one this size.

NORA: What have you called it?

MRS PARADOCK: To tell you the truth, Nora, we haven't called it anything yet. [BRO, *still held firmly by the collar, has a barely perceptible spasm.*] We've hardly had time to get round to discussing names at all, and when we do we only seem to quarrel.

NORA: Are you like that too? We quarrel all the time over names.

MRS PARADOCK: Oh yes. We lose all control. Names and food. It's the only thing worth quarrelling about after all, isn't it?

NORA: Every animal we've ever had all the time we've been here has been called 'Retreat from Moscow', whether it's been the one we ordered or not. We just can't agree on anything else, and so every year we end up calling it 'Retreat from Moscow'.

MRS PARADOCK: Never mind, Nora. Perhaps we'll be able to do without animals altogether one of these days.

NORA: What a hope! But I mustn't keep you standing there with Bro. If you could just let him come on to us in about twenty minutes that'll give me time to open the gate at the back.

MRS PARADOCK: Good-bye, then, Nora. We'll be calling in on Sunday, remember.

NORA: Make it as early as you can. Good-bye, Middie.

MRS PARADOCK: Good-bye.

[NORA *goes out and* MRS PARADOCK *closes the door, releasing* BRO PARADOCK *who crosses the room straightening his jacket.*]

MR PARADOCK: What did you mean about that waste-paper basket? Telling her I tried it on.

MRS PARADOCK: Nora knew what I meant. It's just a private joke between us.

MR PARADOCK: I should think so.

MRS PARADOCK: I was surprised at you if it comes to that. Starting her off on all that long rigmarole about hats. You know what always happens whenever we get on to that subject.

MR PARADOCK: I thought most of what she said was very sensible.

MRS PARADOCK: Bringing Uncle Fred into it like that.

MR PARADOCK: There was no need to disparage him in front of her and make everyone feel uncomfortable.

MRS PARADOCK: There was no need to bring Uncle Fred into it in the first place and then leave it to Nora to change the subject.

MR PARADOCK: Change what subject?

MRS PARADOCK: About the waste-paper basket. That was only to get you off Uncle Fred.

MR PARADOCK: I thought you said that was a private joke between the two of you?

MRS PARADOCK: So it was.

MR PARADOCK: I can't for the life of me in that case see how it was Nora changing the subject.

MRS PARADOCK: There's no point in raking over it all again now. I just get tired that's all of hats hats hats every time anyone calls. Especially Nora.

MR PARADOCK: It happened to have been raining.

MRS PARADOCK: I know it happened to have been raining.

MR PARADOCK: Then we can let the matter drop. Where are my gumboots?

MRS PARADOCK: You don't need gumboots to go down the road a few doors with an elephant. Where are your other shoes?

MR PARADOCK: These are my other shoes I've got on.

MRS PARADOCK: And I should come straight back with Mr Trench. We don't want Mrs Stencil asking a lot of questions.

MR PARADOCK: I notice you're all for calling it Mr Trench now you know it's going to somebody else.

MRS PARADOCK: We've been through all this before. For goodness' sake pull yourself together. We shall have the R.S.P.C.A. round while you stand there.

MR PARADOCK: Perhaps we shall. Perhaps we shan't.

[*He goes out.* MIDDIE PARADOCK *sits down at the table with a glossy magazine.*

The lights fade out in the living room and a half-light reveals two cleaners who as they sweep perfunctorily, resting between bouts, are overheard in conversation.]

FIRST CLEANER: I didn't tell you about Len. He goes down the school of building twice a week now, when he's not working.

SECOND CLEANER: There's a lot of chances for them these days. More than what we had when we was their age.

FIRST CLEANER: He misses his darts now he can't go down The Grapes Tuesdays.

SECOND CLEANER: Like Charlie with his wireless.

FIRST CLEANER: He won the darts championship the other week, his team.

SECOND CLEANER: He misses his wireless. He always goes to the cupboard first thing when he gets in off leave. 'Mum,' he says, 'what you done with the soldering iron?' He come home Sunday.

FIRST CLEANER: Len'll have to go soon.

SECOND CLEANER: Goes back Sunday night. He's put in for apprentice fitter but he don't know if he'll hear anything.

FIRST CLEANER: He was talking about getting deferred but I said to him if you get deferred you'll only have it hanging over you.

SECOND CLEANER: Charlie's made one or two pals where he is. They get a bit fed up with all the routine.

FIRST CLEANER: They all do. It's only natural.

SECOND CLEANER: Everything has to be done to orders and that.

FIRST CLEANER: What Len's hoping is he'll get in the Raf. That's what he's started down at the school of building for, so he can say he's done something.

SECOND CLEANER: How's Gran?

FIRST CLEANER: Up and down. She can't get about like she used.

SECOND CLEANER: You heard about Mrs Jarvis?

FIRST CLEANER: Flo told me.

SECOND CLEANER: She'll have his pension but it's not the same.

FIRST CLEANER: Mr Braithwaite went round from the chapel. Spoke very nice. Said to keep praying and that. 'The Lord will provide, Mrs Jarvis' he said.

SECOND CLEANER: He can't give her what Jarvis could.

FIRST CLEANER: Sh! You'll have them dirty old men out the back listening.

SECOND CLEANER: It's true, isn't it? I reckon she'll miss him that way unless she can find somebody else.

FIRST CLEANER: I didn't tell you what old Mrs Croskett told me when she was round Mrs Jarvis's.

SECOND CLEANER: I didn't know she'd been round there.

FIRST CLEANER: She's been round there twice. So's Mrs Blench. They both said you wouldn't have thought there was nothing wrong with him to see him eat the night before, and then next day he came over funny at work.

SECOND CLEANER: Remember last winter when he was down with the gastric and nobody couldn't say what it was?

FIRST CLEANER: I'll tell you when I started putting two and two together a bit – you know he had that great thick overcoat? The one he had for when he was going anywhere? She's got that out, so Mrs Croskett was saying, and she's got all the seams unpicked and she's going to put a bit of felt lining under it after she's cut it up, and make mats out of it.

SECOND CLEANER: Isn't that Else over there coming across?

[MIDDIE PARADOCK *appears as though relaxing off the set.*]

FIRST CLEANER: I didn't know you'd decided to have another go at the stage, Else.

MRS PARADOCK: It's only while Fred's on night work. I thought I'd keep my hand in. I never expected to see you here though.

SECOND CLEANER: You used to be all for gay parts.

MRS PARADOCK: This one's not so bad. It makes a change.

SECOND CLEANER: I don't know how you can remember your lines – it sounds like a lot of rigmarole to me.

FIRST CLEANER: Everything's that trend nowadays.

MRS PARADOCK: It's all right if you don't think about it. A lot of it's supposed to be symbolic, but you get used to it.

SECOND CLEANER: I don't know, I'm sure.

FIRST CLEANER: How's Fred, Else?

MRS PARADOCK: Fred's fine, thanks, Mrs Gride. We're going down the tabernacle Sundays now. There's a new man there. Mr Brice. Took Mr Jabez' place Christmas. He gets a good crowd Sunday evenings.

SECOND CLEANER: That's nice.

MRS PARADOCK: Fred's very taken with him. We're going to go to the midweek service when he's on early turn if I can get away.

FIRST CLEANER: Wasn't Edie telling us about a Mr Brice?

MRS PARADOCK: We saw Edie there Sunday. He was ever so good on What the Church Means to Me. He's going through all different aspects: at home, you know, and at work and that. Next week it's What the Church Means to Me on Holiday. He gets a lot going up to the mercy seat every Sunday. Fred was on at me to go up but I had my old coat on.

SECOND CLEANER: You feel everybody's looking at you like when Mrs Leakey stood up and give testimony that time we had the women's meeting in the Temperance Hall.

FIRST CLEANER: The Temperance Hall was when we went down Eastbourne with the outing.

SECOND CLEANER: That's right. Surely you remember Mrs Leakey? Kep' on all the way back in the coach about she's saved, she's saved all the time.

MRS PARADOCK: It's the thanksgiving Sunday week. Why don't you and Mrs Gride come over?

SECOND CLEANER: We'll see what the weather does, Else dear. It's a long way with my legs – the journey knocks me over.

FIRST CLEANER [nodding towards the set]: You look as if you're wanted, Else.

MRS PARADOCK [waves her hand]: It's only Sam but I suppose I'd better go. Must be time. I expect you'll both be gone by the time I'm finished so I'll say good-bye. Good-bye, Mrs Gride. Remember me to Len. Good-bye, Mrs Quiller.

[She goes back to the set, which remains in darkness. The rest of the stage remains dimly lit. A spotlight is turned on to the cleaners.]

FIRST CLEANER: Goodness! They've turned the lights on us!

SECOND CLEANER: That'll be Bert's idea of a joke.

[They gather up buckets and mops and hustle each other out.]

SECOND CLEANER: They've properly caught us with our trousers down.

FIRST CLEANER: Sh! You'll have us locked up!

[*Blackout. Lights in set go up.* MIDDIE PARADOCK *is sitting at the table reading a glossy magazine.*

She puts it away, and begins a game of patience.]

MRS PARADOCK [*without looking up*]: Come in.

[*She continues in thought, places two more cards on the table, looks towards the door, and repeats 'Come in'. When nothing happens she impatiently puts down the cards and goes to the door. As she opens it to find no one there, the two* COMEDIANS *enter by the door behind her, sit at the table and continue the game of patience. She turns away from the door, closing it, and speaks half to herself, and half to the two at the table, whose presence she takes for granted.*]

MRS PARADOCK: I made sure that was somebody at the door.

[*She stands for a moment watching the game.*]

MRS PARADOCK: Don't you two ever get tired of patience?

FIRST COMEDIAN: We've been drinking again, Mrs Paradock.

MRS PARADOCK: So you've taken my advice, have you?

SECOND COMEDIAN: We feel a whole lot tipsier for it.

MRS PARADOCK: Isn't that what I told you? You never listen to me.

SECOND COMEDIAN: It was that delicious ambrosia you gave us when we were here last week, Mrs Paradock. That was what put us on to drinking.

MRS PARADOCK: It's a very stimulating drink. Bro and I keep coming back to it and the surprising thing is we're always finding something fresh to make us drunk in it. I'm glad you both like it.

FIRST COMEDIAN: We've gone on to other things since, of course. What was it we were drinking last week-end? Bug said he couldn't remember when a drink left him so well oiled.

SECOND COMEDIAN: Raven's Blood – but I thought the name was the weakest part of it. What I enjoyed was the glass in the middle of the bottle. I spent a long time over that – just savouring it.

MRS PARADOCK: Bro's in the middle of a good bottle now. I'll get him to pour you out drops of it when he comes in.

FIRST COMEDIAN: Where is Bro, Mrs Paradock?

MRS PARADOCK: He's out with an elephant, but he should be back. We had one delivered that was too big for what we want, so we've done a sort of switch with Mrs Mortice. She's left us this snake.

[*Takes down pencil box from shelf*] And Bro's taking our elephant round to her. [*Opens box.*]

FIRST COMEDIAN: It looks hardly long enough for a snake.

MRS PARADOCK: You can have them lengthened but we shan't bother.

SECOND COMEDIAN: I think snakes are too long for what you generally want them for. People just like to go one better than everybody else.

MRS PARADOCK [*glances out through the window*]: Here's Bro now. [*She goes to open the door.*] You've been a long time.

[BRO PARADOCK *comes in, swaying a little, but otherwise normal in his manner.*]

MR PARADOCK: I've been in the pub on my way back. Hallo, Bug. Hallo, Hamster, old boy. I got stuck into a bottle in the pub and I couldn't tear myself away. I'm trying to remember what it was called. You two would enjoy it.

MRS PARADOCK: You look as if you've been having a good old drink, doesn't he, Bug? His eyes are all bloodshot. . . .

SECOND COMEDIAN: I think Mrs Paradock is the only one of us who – [*Pause.*]

MRS PARADOCK: Finish what you were going to say, Bug.

SECOND COMEDIAN: No, I'd rather leave it at that, Mrs Paradock.

MR PARADOCK: You were in the middle of a sentence, for God's sake!

FIRST COMEDIAN: He does that sometimes. He often leaves a sentence unfinished. It's more effective. It's like a sawn-off shotgun.

MRS PARADOCK [*grimacing*]: I don't like the sound of that remark.

MR PARADOCK: What's wrong with it?

MRS PARADOCK: I don't like the sound of it. It sounds as if it's on the turn to me.

MR PARADOCK: It would have turned before now if it was going to turn.

SECOND COMEDIAN: It's only the sound of it, Mrs Paradock.

MRS PARADOCK: That remark will be paradoxical tomorrow morning when it comes out of the subconscious. You can't tell me anything about paradoxes.

FIRST COMEDIAN: Reminds me of an old stage designer who after a lifetime of faking stage props to look genuine had to admit defeat for the first time when he had to fake something to look bogus.

SECOND COMEDIAN: Talking about paradoxes, what about the platoon sergeant who sent his men into a wood to take cover and when they got there, said: 'You can take it easy, now, lads. We're out of the wood!'

MRS PARADOCK: You men. You're all as bad as one another, with your horrible paradoxes.

MR PARADOCK: Let's put the case of someone forgetting his lines on the stage at the exact point where he's supposed in the play to pretend to have forgotten them.

FIRST COMEDIAN: I don't think I follow. You're a bit too drunk for me.

MR PARADOCK: He has to give the illusion that he's forgotten his lines. As part of the play. All right?

FIRST COMEDIAN: Yes. I follow that.

MR PARADOCK: Now. At the precise moment when he's supposed to give the illusion of having forgotten his lines he quite forgets what it is he has to do. His mind goes blank. So what happens? There's a pause. The pause prolongs itself. But sooner or later he remembers what it is he ought to have been doing. He ought to have been giving the impression of having been at a loss for words. There's nothing he can do about it now. The audience will have to make do with the reality instead of the illusion – which would probably have been much better. They might well have had to do without both. He might well have forgotten not only that he was supposed to stumble for words, but that there was anything he was supposed to do at all. In that case he'd have gone straight on – word-perfect. Thus – the illusion of having remembered may be sustained only by forgetting, and the illusion of having forgotten only by remembering.

MRS PARADOCK: I've only one thing against these paradoxes. They're like puns – they're just plays on words when you analyse them. I don't mind good, solid, practical puns. I don't mind a pun in real life that means something. In fact I like to see somebody using his boot as a hammer, for instance. That's a practical pun.

MR PARADOCK: That can be carried too far as well.

SECOND COMEDIAN: Hamster's brother-in-law's a great practical punster. I remember the time he threw a vase at a cat. It was a beauty. It did as much damage as a genuine missile and he used it to put flowers in afterwards.

[*A knock.* MIDDIE PARADOCK *goes out.*]

MR PARADOCK: It's a pity you can't use an umbrella-stand in the breech of a fifteen-inch naval gun. If you could I should feel a whole lot happier about using a shell-case as a doorstop.

FIRST COMEDIAN: That's life, Bro. It's no use looking for an editorial in a tablecloth simply because you eat your meals off a newspaper.

[MIDDIE PARADOCK *comes in with an opened telegram which she is reading.*]

MRS PARADOCK: It's Don and that motor scooter again. I shall be glad when we see the last of that craze.

MR PARADOCK: What's he up to this time?

MRS PARADOCK: Read it. [*Hands the telegram to* BRO. *To others.*] He's been parking his motor scooter on that piece of waste ground again behind Rachmaninov's Second Piano Concerto.

MR PARADOCK: Who does that belong to?

MRS PARADOCK: It doesn't belong to anybody. It's just a piece of waste ground.

MR PARADOCK: Then they can't stop him parking his motor scooter on it if it doesn't belong to anyone.

SECOND COMEDIAN: What does the telegram say, Mrs Paradock?

MR PARADOCK [*He is still holding the telegram.*]: Arriving twelve-ten Euston send sandwiches. [*Hands the telegram to* SECOND COMEDIAN.]

FIRST COMEDIAN: I shouldn't let that upset you, Mrs Paradock. It doesn't mean what it says.

MR PARADOCK: The last time we had a telegram like this it was worded very differently.

FIRST COMEDIAN: I should just say nothing about the motor

scooter. Say nothing to him about it. When he's gone to bed perhaps you can find a salesman to sell it to.

MRS PARADOCK: I doubt it. He bought it from a buyer.

SECOND COMEDIAN: You can set your minds at rest about the telegram. It's in code.

MRS PARADOCK: Thank heaven for that.

MR PARADOCK: How can you tell it's in code?

SECOND COMEDIAN: There's no way of telling, I'm afraid. It either is or it isn't. This one is.

FIRST COMEDIAN: I thought it was from the beginning. The moment Mrs Paradock came in with it. You can always tell with a telegram. As Bug says, it's either in code or it isn't.

[The door opens. DON, a smartly dressed woman in her twenties, comes in.]

SECOND COMEDIAN: Here's Don now.

MRS PARADOCK: Don! Why, you've changed your sex!

DON: Didn't you get my telegram?

MR PARADOCK: We got it all right, but it was in code.

DON: It shouldn't have been. I asked them to decode it before they sent it off.

MRS PARADOCK: Never mind. I always wanted a girl.

MR PARADOCK: That's the first I knew of it.

FIRST COMEDIAN: Now perhaps we can have that conversation we promised ourselves about the conversation we had at the Wordsworths'.

MRS PARADOCK: So we can. I've been waiting to hear all about it. I expect Don there's feeling like a good long conversation after travelling up to Euston since four o'clock this morning. What were the trains like this time, Don?

DON: Don't talk about them, Mother. One long compartment after another.

MR PARADOCK: Well, let's start this conversation. How was it we broke the ice at the Wordsworths'? What was it we began with? A noun clause each, wasn't it?

DON: That's right. We were all given a noun clause each – in apposition – and then we had to go round asking everyone in turn for the noun it was in apposition to, till we found the right one.

MRS PARADOCK: I suppose John was as much in demand as ever with his adverbial clauses?

DON: Oh, John! John's got a thing about his adverbial clauses.

FIRST COMEDIAN: He can be a bit childish about them too at times. Over those subordinating conjunctions, for instance, that he said were prepositions.

DON: That was Margaret. What actually happened was that he asked for subordinating conjunctions and she handed him these prepositions thinking they were adverbs or something.

SECOND COMEDIAN: And then to make matters worse she said, 'Will these do? I can never tell the difference myself'.

FIRST COMEDIAN: 'I can never tell the difference'! What a thing to say to John of all people.

DON: You know that little spot of high colour he gets on the side of his forehead whenever he's annoyed at anything. . . .

FIRST COMEDIAN: Annoyed! It was all he could do to be civil to her. [BRO PARADOCK *stands apart from the others staring tight-lipped into the distance.*]

SECOND COMEDIAN: Tell them about Joe, Hamster.

FIRST COMEDIAN: Joe?

DON: And the figures of speech.

FIRST COMEDIAN: Oh. 'Give me good plain syntax', you mean? I don't think he'd met half the figures of speech before.

SECOND COMEDIAN: I happened to look up when someone put that synecdoche in front of him. 'What's this?' he said. 'Metonymy?'

FIRST COMEDIAN: Metonymy!

DON: What about Mrs Kapellmeister then? Falling over herself almost for a transferred epithet every time one appeared. I suppose she was afraid someone else might get to them first.

MRS PARADOCK: Looking at her husband sometimes, I'm surprised to hear she didn't go for oxymoron. I've never seen anyone who looks more like the original sustained metaphor than he does.

DON: He's certainly at the opposite end of the pole from her.

MRS PARADOX: It's only zeugma that keeps them together. [*She goes across to where* BRO PARADOCK *is still morosely standing, while the others continue talking amongst themselves.*] What's the matter with you? Moping over here on your own?

MR PARADOCK: There's nothing the matter with me at all.

MRS PARADOCK: Why can't you join in the conversation then? Standing here saying nothing.

MR PARADOCK: I'm standing here saying nothing because I can't think of anything to say. I should have thought that was obvious.

MRS PARADOCK: Can't think of anything to say! Surely you could define 'consanguinity' or something.

MR PARADOCK: What chance have I had to define 'consanguinity'?

MRS PARADOCK: You've had just as much chance as anybody else. For goodness' sake come and join in the conversation even if it's only to contradict somebody.

MR PARADOCK [*reluctantly, and with the look of a martyr, he goes towards the others*]: My wife wants me to take part in the conversation.

SECOND COMEDIAN: We were just saying what a good party it was, by and large.

DON: It would have been if that girl with coordinate clause written all over her face hadn't tried to monopolize Max all evening.

FIRST COMEDIAN: At least we were spared Charles this time with his endless paronomasia.

DON: I'd rather have Charles than that one with the dreary onomatopoeia who was doing farmyard imitations with it every five minutes.

FIRST COMEDIAN: Oh no. Not farmyard imitations?

DON: He was. I thought he was never going to stop and then when Margaret asked him if he ever added to his repertoire and he did half a dozen new ones I could have killed her. It was only the thought of her adverbial clauses of concession that stopped me, I think.

SECOND COMEDIAN: I can't say they impressed me all that much. They've nothing like the sheer architectonic qualities, for instance, of successive adjectival clauses one on top of another in the hands of a master.

MR PARADOCK: Architectonic archbishops! I could give you some adjectival clauses that would scorch the seat off your pants to listen to them [*Loudly*]: This is the soldier that loved the wife that poisoned the hangman that hanged the murderer that shot the assassin that stabbed the king that won the war that killed the soldier that loved the wife that poisoned the hangman that hanged the murderer that shot the assassin that stabbed the king that won the war that killed the soldier that loved the wife that . . .

MRS PARADOCK: For goodness' sake pull yourself together! It's in bad taste. Can't you forget you're an undertaker once in a while?

SECOND COMEDIAN: I never knew Bro was an undertaker.

FIRST COMEDIAN: Neither did I. I'd noticed he was always rather partial to death. Now I see why.

MRS PARADOCK: It's his life.

MR PARADOCK: It's just that I see things from an undertaker's point of view.

MRS PARADOCK: There's no need to make everyone feel uncomfortable just because you can't arrive at a definition of 'consanguinity'. He's set his mind on defining 'consanguinity' and there's no shifting him. Everyone else has to take second place when he's in this mood.

MR PARADOCK: All I want is a chance to define *something*. It doesn't have to be 'consanguinity'. That was your suggestion. It isn't as if I often get the time for defining things.

MRS PARADOCK: Or the inclination.

FIRST COMEDIAN: I think we'd better be off, Bug. Remember you're expecting a phone call at nine o'clock.

SECOND COMEDIAN: She rang this morning. [FIRST COMEDIAN *nudges him.*] She'll be ringing me again though at nine o'clock. I wasn't in this morning. No one answered the phone.

FIRST COMEDIAN: Good-bye, Mrs Paradock.

MRS PARADOCK: You're not going?

FIRST COMEDIAN: Bug's got a phone call he's expecting and I ought to be getting back to my filing.

MRS PARADOCK [*out of Bro's hearing*]: He'll be all right tomorrow.

SECOND COMEDIAN: We'll look in, Mrs Paradock, and see how he is.

DON: Don't you worry about father. We'll get him to bed with a hot-water bottle.

[*They go out.*]

SECOND COMEDIAN: Good-bye, Mrs Paradock. Good-bye, Bro.

FIRST COMEDIAN: Are you coming out with us, Don?

DON: I've got to go down the road a little way.

FIRST COMEDIAN: Good-bye, Bro. Good-bye, Mrs Paradock.

MRS PARADOCK: Look after yourselves.

[MIDDIE PARADOCK *closes the door and turns to Bro.*]

MRS PARADOCK: A fine exhibition you made of yourself.

MR PARADOCK: Where's Don?

MRS PARADOCK: Gone where you can't harm her any more with your bitter words.

MR PARADOCK: I think I'll have a turn in the garden.

MRS PARADOCK: We haven't got a garden. You know that as well as I do.

MR PARADOCK: I understood we had. It's in the deeds.

MRS PARADOCK: Is it?

MR PARADOCK: I wouldn't have bought the house otherwise.

MRS PARADOCK: House? This is a bungalow.

MR PARADOCK: I wouldn't have bought it without looking pretty closely at the deeds to see if there was any mention of a garden.

MRS PARADOCK: If you can find a garden in the deeds of this place you're welcome to take a turn in it.

[*There is a pause while Bro ponders this.*]

MRS PARADOCK: I should get up to bed if I were you.

MR PARADOCK: *Up* to bed? I thought we were living in a bungalow?

MRS PARADOCK: Look, Bro. I'm trying to help you. You're being very difficult and perverse and I'm trying very hard to be reasonable with you and understand you. Don't forget I'm just as drunk as you are underneath and I'm trying to fight it for both of us. You don't make it very easy for me, Bro.

MR PARADOCK: I didn't know you were drunk too. I thought it was just me.

MRS PARADOCK: You never do think it's ever possible for me to feel a bit blotto from time to time, Bro. You think you're the only one who takes a pull at the bottle occasionally.

MR PARADOCK: I sometimes envy the man in the street who's never learned to drink for himself at all.

MRS PARADOCK: It's no good getting cynical, Bro.

MR PARADOCK: I do get cynical sometimes. The average man seems to be quite content to let the rest of us do all his drinking for him.

MRS PARADOCK: That's true, Bro, but although he's spared a lot of the hangovers, don't forget that he misses the intoxication too.

MR PARADOCK: Perhaps you're right, Middie, my dear.

MRS PARADOCK: And now we must get out of here, Bro, because the producer wants it for his critics' meeting or something in a few minutes. So up you get.

[*She helps him out. Lights fade out. Author's mouthpiece appears to right of set.*]

AUTHOR: It seemed the only way. I think we have all been trying as hard as can reasonably be expected not to show our exasperation – I certainly have – because we do all like, naturally, to feel we've been provided with a meaning; something we can carry round with us like an umbrella for a few days. We all feel rather lost without a meaning to seize hold of; rather like a snake charmer in front of a boa constrictor and no flute. Or whatever they use. And in this search for a meaning we have some very good allies in the critics. They know a great deal about these things. They are trained to find meanings, and even if there are no meanings to be found they rarely come unprovided with spare meanings which with a little wire and string can often be fastened quite securely. So it is to the critics that for all our sakes I have decided to turn. We've got to turn somewhere. And what help I could have given you would have been worse than useless. I lay claim to no special vision and my own notions as to what it is I have in mind here may well fall pitifully short of your own far better notions. No. I am the dwarf in the circus – I give what scope I can to such deficiencies as I have. Beyond that, it is to these public servants of ours who guide us all to destinations (which even though they may not always amount to very much as destinations are nevertheless the best

destinations we have), it is to the critics that we must commit ourselves. But for them we would be hard put to it to arrive anywhere
at all. And it's the arriving somewhere which gives us the illusion
that the journey has been worth while. No such illusion is likely to
trouble any of us here, but perhaps we need not go home altogether
empty-handed for all that – because here they are. Here is the first
of the critics. This is, I need hardly tell you, a very welcome sight.
I think we are shortly going to be led out of the wilderness. It's
Mustard Short, you've probably recognized him, who has just
taken his seat.

[*The critics as they arrive sit down round the table in the living room.*
MUSTARD SHORT *is the first to arrive, but is closely followed by*
DENZIL PEPPER *who takes a chair opposite him. When* MISS SALT
and MRS VINEGAR *come in together they occupy the remaining seats,
leaving a seat vacant at the head of the table for the Chairman.*]

It was Mustard Short as you know who last year – or was it earlier
than that, in some previous incarnation perhaps? – who drew
attention to some faults of structure in *Tristram Shandy*. And here
is Denzil Pepper, carrying his high standards invisibly in brown
paper, manœuvring them clear of the light fittings and as ready
devastatingly to unwrap them here as anywhere else. 'If this
weren't in a bucket', he roars, getting a lump of soap and plunging
his hands into a bucket of sulphuric acid, 'if this weren't in a
bucket, I should never have guessed it was meant to be water!'
He's the boy. He's the one, if anybody can, who'll unmask the
shadow. In a bloody froth of fulmination, too, unless he happens
to have taken a sedative. Mrs Vinegar there – she's the woman in
the black suit who has just sat down on the left of Mustard Short
– looks, I must say, disconcertingly the worse for tedium. Miss
Salt on the other hand is clearly ready to begin digging with
indefatigable trowel among whatever unfruitful clods of dramatic
earth she finds at her dedicated feet, and may, for all we can tell,
come upon something which will surprise us all. And now let us
alert the coastguards of our minds, for the Chairman has arrived.
We must try now to assume receptive postures, and be ready to give
asylum to such thoughts as are shortly to come among us.

[*Lights, except in the living room, fade.*]

CHAIRMAN [*standing*]: Shall we ask a blessing? [*All stand.*] For what
we are now about to bestow may we be made truly worthy.

MISS SALT: I protest!

PEPPER: I deplore!

MUSTARD: I condemn!

MRS VINEGAR: I denounce!

MISS SALT: I wish to go on record as having cringed.

PEPPER: I wish to go on record as having writhed.

MUSTARD: I wish to go on record as having squirmed.

MRS VINEGAR: I wish to go on record as having suffered agony.

MISS SALT: I hail!

PEPPER: I salute!

MUSTARD: I predict!

MRS VINEGAR: I acclaim!

ALL [*loudly and in unison*]: I wish to go on record! I wish to go on
record! I wish to go on record! [*Sit.*]

CHAIRMAN: We'll start at once with a discussion of the performance
we have all been watching for the last hour or so, and we'll begin
by deciding if we can what it is we have been present at, before
going on to a consideration of its merits. Is this piece the bold
experiment some people hold it to be? Is it a shameless plagiarism
from the pen of a true primitive of the theatre – as someone has
said – or is it neither of these things? Denzil Pepper – what do you
make of this?

PEPPER: This is a hotch-potch. I think that emerges quite clearly. The
thing has been thrown together – a veritable rag-bag of last year's
damp fireworks, if a mixed metaphor is in order.

MISS SALT: Yes. I suppose it *is* what we must call a hotch-potch. I
do think, though – accepting Denzil Pepper's definition – I do
think, and this is the point I feel we ought to make, it is, surely,
isn't it, an *inspired* hotch-potch?

PEPPER: A hotch-potch de luxe. Only the finest ingredients. A
theatrical haggis.

CHAIRMAN: Isn't this what our ancestors would have delighted in
calling a gallimaufry?

[*Pause.*]

MUSTARD: 'They have made our English tongue a gallimaufry or hodgepodge of all other speeches.' Yes. The letter to Gabriel Harvey at the beginning of Spenser's Shepherd's Calendar. Yes. I'm not sure that I don't prefer the word gallimaufry to Denzil Pepper's hodgepodge.

PEPPER: Hotch-potch. No. I stick, quite unrepentantly, to my own word.

MISS SALT: I'm wondering whether what Spenser was saying there was not referring to the language itself rather than to what was said in it? Words and phrases borrowed from other languages and so on? I think perhaps – and I say this under correction: I know Mustard Short is more familiar than I am *with* the attitude to this kind of thing in James Joyce – isn't this . . . haven't we got here an actual *repudiation* on the Joycean model *of* orderliness in a way the writers Spenser was attacking had not?

PEPPER: I'm not at all happy about letting him get away with it on his own terms like that. After all, what happens when a boxer gets knocked out in the ring? He's lost the fight. It's as simple as that. He's lost the fight and it makes no difference that his manager or someone announces through the loudspeaker afterwards that lying flat on his back was a deliberate repudiation of the vertical.

MRS VINEGAR: I couldn't agree more.

CHAIRMAN: Mrs Vinegar.

MRS VINEGAR: I was bored with this play. Or whatever it is. I was bored almost from the rise of the curtain with the characters – or is characters too strong a word? – and I was even more bored by the situations they were put into.

MUSTARD: And the acting? Were you bored with the acting? I thought the cast carried it off for him exceptionally well.

PEPPER: A splendid cast.

MUSTARD: Quite exceptionally well.

MISS SALT: It was in fact an actors' play.

MUSTARD: An actors' play and of course in a way a producer's play.

CHAIRMAN: How would Mrs Vinegar feel about calling this an actors' play?

MRS VINEGAR: No. No, I thought the acting was extremely good. The production I'm less sure about, but it was quite sound. As for this being an actors' play or a producer's play, whatever that may mean, I think fifth-rate play is the only sound designation for it. No amount of talent on the stage can make a fifth-rate play into a third-rate one, although it was quite obvious that that was what they were aiming at.

CHAIRMAN: Mustard Short. Were you bored by this play?

MUSTARD: Bored, no. Exasperated at times, yes. I did, I think, suppress a mild yawn twice, but I smiled occasionally, wondered what was coming next, got annoyed and irritated fairly frequently – in fact reacted much as one does in the theatre, except for experiencing tension. There was no tension and no tears. That I think was a pity because with so much else there it would have been nice for the sake of completeness to have had those as well.

MRS VINEGAR: May I ask Mustard why, if he felt a genuine desire to yawn, he suppressed it?

MUSTARD: Politeness, I suppose – it's a vice we're all prone to in the theatre, where we could do with a lot less of it.

MISS SALT: If only to keep Aunt Edna in Surbiton.

MRS VINEGAR: The way to keep Aunt Edna or anybody else in Surbiton is to go on putting on plays like this one. And in that event I shall be in Surbiton too, I hope.

CHAIRMAN: We seem to be getting away from the play itself. Can we try to reach agreement on what kind of production this is? Is it a comedy? The play has a sub-title: The Accapictor Michmacted – A Comedy. Denzil Pepper – what do you think about this play as a comedy?

PEPPER: What do I think about it as a comedy? I believe I laughed once. So, technically, I suppose the play could be called a comedy.

MRS VINEGAR: As a matter of curiosity – what was it Denzil Pepper laughed at?

PEPPER: I really can't remember what it was.

MUSTARD: Perhaps calling it a comedy is part of the comedy?

PEPPER: Perhaps so. If someone had told me that, I would certainly have done what I could to laugh. But that's just what I'm never quite sure about – what *is* it we're being asked to do here? Are we being asked to laugh at him, laugh with him – or are we meant, God forbid, to take him seriously?

MUSTARD: It's satire, surely.

MISS SALT: What was it Swift called satire? A mirror, wasn't it, in which a man sees any face but his own. It's certainly very true here.

MUSTARD: 'Satire is a sort of glass, wherein beholders do generally discover everybody's face but their own.'

PEPPER: I would have been delighted to have caught a glimpse even of my own face!

MISS SALT: Oh, the face was there. It was impossible at times to identify it, even to distinguish it – it will take a careful reading and re-reading of the play to do that – but the face was there. Of that I'm quite certain.

CHAIRMAN: Did you, Mustard Short, discover a face you could recognize?

MUSTARD: None, I'm afraid. None whatever.

MISS SALT: A contorted face, perhaps? I thought I saw that. The human face. In the human predicament. Contorted with grief? With pain?

MRS VINEGAR: With boredom.

MUSTARD: Could he, I wonder, be satirizing satire?

CHAIRMAN: A skit on satire itself. How does that strike you, Miss Salt?

MISS SALT: Yes. Yes, I think it very likely. I'm wondering whether perhaps rather than skit the word parody would hit off better what it is he's trying for here. Could he be parodying the whole thing? The whole concept? A parody *of* a skit, if that's possible.

PEPPER: If this is a parody of a skit at all, it must be a parody of a skit *on* something.

MUSTARD: A parody of a skit on satire?

PEPPER: For a sophisticated audience. It goes without saying that it's a sophisticated audience he's got in mind here. I take it that's agreed.

MUSTARD: A sophisticated audience.

MRS VINEGAR: A sophisticated audience flagging.

MUSTARD: No. I think if I may say so Mrs Vinegar is being rather too uncompromisingly hostile to what is – let us be as fair as we possibly can about it – to what is by any standards a remarkable . . . a remarkable phenomenon.

MISS SALT: I'd rather like to take up this idea of the skit again, or the parody of it, because – and this is surely the whole point which none of us has made yet – here is a play in which the writer is imitating himself repeatedly all through the play. He is in fact actually burlesquing his own self-mimicry and in quite the most devastating way from first to last. That I think is inherent in the whole thing.

PEPPER: He's satirizing farce, of course, too. That comes across quite unmistakably. As one of the characters says somewhere in the play – this is the custard-pie farce of the intellect.

MUSTARD: Comedy. Custard-pie comedy. Of the abstract. But to get back to this point about burlesque. It is, basically, a parody of a skit on satire that he's burlesquing, and the farce is so to speak a by-product of that. I don't think he's aiming at farce at all. The farce is in a sense what we, the audience, *contribute*.

CHAIRMAN: The audience. Did anyone else, I wonder, feel – as I certainly did – that the barrier between audience and actors was being quite deliberately dismantled? Mrs Vinegar?

MRS VINEGAR: It's been done before. And done better.

MUSTARD: You mean the *Verfremdungseffekt*. The alienation effect.

MISS SALT: It's Brecht, of course – though with a very different aim from that of Brecht.

PEPPER: No. I don't see Brecht here at all.

MISS SALT: It's the Brechtian technique carried on *beyond* Brecht. Isn't that it?

MUSTARD: Beyond, and in a sense of course at a tangent to Brecht. It's as though he'd gone off on a branch line some way back which is carrying him farther than Brecht was able to go but in a quite different direction.

MISS SALT: And, of course, *facing* Brecht as he moves away from him. The farther he goes *beyond* Brecht, therefore, the farther he is retreating *from* him.

PEPPER: I can accept Brecht as starting-point. But a starting-point i
something you move away from, and in my view the author of thi
play has been doing just that. He has been putting more and mor
ground between himself and his model – if that's what Brecht is
though I doubt it – and they have been getting farther and farthe
apart, these two, until both of them are specks on the horizon
Which is why I think we're quite wrong to be discussing this play
or whatever it is as if it were The Comedy of Errors rewritten by
Lewis Carroll to provide a part for Godot or somebody.

CHAIRMAN: Yes. Well, now our time is running out and I think we
ought to say something about the ending – which we've none of u
yet seen of course. Is it possible that some of the shortcomings of the
play so far could be redeemed by the ending? Mrs Vinegar.

MRS VINEGAR: I doubt whether I could sit through any more of it. I
have never begrudged danger money to steeplejacks and people of
that kind, and I do think it's high time someone suggested boredom
money for critics. The ending? No. I think the piece is beyond
redemption. The best that can be hoped for from the ending is that
sooner or later it will arrive.

CHAIRMAN: Denzil Pepper. What do you think about the ending?

PEPPER: I think it's the Russians, isn't it, who have a proverb to the
effect that if you can't hold a horse by the mane, you'll never hold
it by the tail?

[Pause.]

MUSTARD: You can count all the same on being dragged a reasonable
distance before having to let go.

PEPPER: Possibly. I'm not sure, though, that I want to do my travelling at the tail of a runaway horse.

MRS VINEGAR: Is it travelling along the road of life we're talking
about? Because, as far as that journey is concerned, I broke the back
of it this evening during the first act.

CHAIRMAN: And that I'm afraid will have to end the discussion if not
the play, because our time is up. I'm sorry to have to apply the
guillotine to a discussion which has been so lively – I think we've
rarely had a livelier discussion of any play. And a play which can
stimulate as much strong feeling, or even boredom! [laughter] is

something we can always do with in the theatre. I'm sure we would all of us agree, whatever our individual reactions to it may have been, that we have here a play the real author of which will not be born for many years to come.

ALL: Hear, hear.

[*The light in the living room fades. A half-light reveals the author's mouthpiece, who is sitting on a chair staring ahead with a quite blank expression. He starts convulsively, stands up, and looks, with no change of expression, towards the audience. As the lights come up in the living room, revealing* BRO PARADOCK *sitting with a newspaper before him, the author's mouthpiece glances quickly in that direction, and then goes slowly out as though dazed.*

The scene is exactly the same as in Act One, Scene I. MIDDIE PARADOCK *comes into the room and begins tidying it, speaking as she does so.*]

MRS PARADOCK: There's somebody at the door wanting you to form a government.

MR PARADOCK: When?

MRS PARADOCK: He says he's working through the street directory. He's waiting outside now.

MR PARADOCK: What does he look like?

MRS PARADOCK: In an old raincoat. He's probably trying it on. I shall want this cork opened in case we have to offer him a drink.

MR PARADOCK: It's nectar if it's anything. Not ambrosia.

MRS PARADOCK: He won't be able to tell the difference.

MR PARADOCK: If he can't tell the difference between ambrosia and nectar he shouldn't be wearing an old raincoat.

MRS PARADOCK: He's only trying it on for size. I got that much out of him.

MR PARADOCK: In that case what does he want me to form a government for?

MRS PARADOCK: I should have thought that was obvious.

MR PARADOCK: Supposing it turns out to be Uncle Ted having a joke?

MRS PARADOCK: You know as well as I do Uncle Ted hasn't got a sense of humour any longer.

MR PARADOCK: He may think I look like Gladstone.

MRS PARADOCK: What if he does? You've got a good many year in front of you yet.

MR PARADOCK: Don't start on that, Middie, please.

MRS PARADOCK: You're in your prime.

MR PARADOCK: Middie!

MRS PARADOCK: A man with your constitution at your time of life is in for a good long spell of it yet.

MR PARADOCK: Can't you leave me alone, Middie? Can't you keep quiet about it?

MRS PARADOCK: You're as fit as you've ever been.

MR PARADOCK: Stop baiting me, Middie! Just shut up about being in my prime. You only keep on about it because you know it plays merry hell with my death wish!

[*Black-out. Enter, in front of living room set, a* MAN IN A BOWLER HAT *carrying a manuscript case.*]

MAN IN BOWLER HAT: Who's in charge here? Where's the producer or somebody?

[*Enter* PRODUCER *from right.*]

They've had about as much as they can take of this out there. [*To audience*] I don't know how you feel about my breaking in on the production like this, but [*to Producer*] I think we've all had about enough.

PRODUCER: You think the curtain ought to come down, sir?

MAN IN BOWLER HAT: It's unpleasant for everyone when an audience begins to get restive. [*To audience*] I know that only too well from an experience of my own when I was foolish enough on one occasion to consent to act as chairman at a political meeting of all things. The member was speaking – or rather not the member, because as it turned out he lost his deposit – but the candidate as he was then was speaking at the time and some unruly elements . . .

[*Enter from right* AUTHOR *in high spirits.*]

AUTHOR: Well. What a waste of talent it's all been! What a waste!

MAN IN BOWLER HAT [*in sotto voce panic*]: *Pas devant les auditeurs!*

AUTHOR: *Les auditeurs.* I must say they've all for the most part taken insult after insult in a splendid spirit. Don't you think so?

ACT TWO

PRODUCER: They've taken it very well. But I think perhaps we ought to try and get the curtain down. They'll be wanting to get away.

AUTHOR: I'll have a little chat with them. Take Henry Irving with you and get working on the curtain – it's probably jammed.

[PRODUCER *and* MAN IN BOWLER HAT *go out right.*]

AUTHOR: It's been an odd evening to say the least of it. I don't quite know whether it would be arrogant of me to take the blame on the grounds that it was I who initiated it all – or whether perhaps we ought all to share bouquets and brickbats promiscuously among us. My own contribution probably seems more important than it is because, as I say, it was my small contribution which set it all going as it were – and yet, if it comes to that, which of you with a shot or two of benzedrine couldn't have done as well or better? But there is an important point which may be overlooked unless I draw attention to it now and it's this: The retreat from reason means precious little to anyone who has never caught up with reason in the first place. It takes a trained mind to relish a *non sequitur.* So you can take comfort from that. And now one last thing. This is a delicate subject to broach but . . . we on this side of the footlights feel that some gesture from us would be more than appropriate in view of . . . of your forbearance, but on the other hand we felt that anything we might do by way of applauding the audience would seem somehow to smack if not of affectation at any rate of . . . the unconventional? We don't want to fly in the face of tradition but . . .

[*Lights come up in the living room set where the cast is assembled. Each holds a glass of a bright, purple liquid ready to respond to a toast.*]

AUTHOR: The audience!

ALL: The audience!

[*They drink.*]

CURTAIN